What Every Middle School Teacher Needs to Know About Reading Tests

(From Someone Who Has Written Them)

Charles Fuhrken

Stenhouse Publishers
Portland, Maine

D1509766

Stenhouse Publishers
www.stenhouse.com

Credits
Page 110: "No Matter Where We've Been" by Walt McDonald, *Texas Co-Op Power Magazine*, February 2005.
Page 119: Excerpted from "Bad Sports" by Melissa Gaskill, *Texas Co-Op Power Magazine*, August 2005.

Library of Congress Cataloging-in-Publication Data
Fuhrken, Charles, 1970–
    What every middle school teacher needs to know about reading tests (from someone who has written them) / Charles Fuhrken.
        p. cm.
    Includes bibliographical references and index.
    ISBN 978-1-57110-885-2 (pbk. : alk. paper)—ISBN 978-1-57110-945-3 (ebook) 1. Reading (Middle school)—Ability testing. I. Title.
    LB1632.F84 2011
    428.4071'2—dc23
                                                                            2011037287

Cover design, interior design, and typesetting by Martha Drury
Manufactured in the United States of America
PRINTED ON 30% PCW
    RECYCLED PAPER

18 17 16 15 14 13   9 8 7 6 5 4 3 2

To the teachers who made a reader and writer of me, and to middle school teachers everywhere who keep books in kids' hands

Contents

Acknowledgments

I am so appreciative that my first book about reading assessments, *What Every Elementary Teacher Needs to Know About Reading Tests* (2009), made possible the forging of many wonderful relationships. New friendships have developed with teachers who found my book "by accident," or were handed a copy by a fellow teacher, or heard me at a conference, or blogged about the book because they want others to know. And teacher educators have found a welcome place for the book in their courses about literacy and assessment. I took from these sources that this new book for middle school teachers will be welcomed. Thanks especially to these new friends as well as some former and present colleagues for their correspondence and support as I worked on this second book about assessment: Kemp Gregory, Nancy Gregory, Amy Koenning, Sybil Lacey, Alana Morris, Nancy Roser, Jennifer Saenz, Alexa Spahr, Elma Torres, and Judy Wallis. Thanks, too, to my mother and sister, who talk about both books to anyone who will listen.

Everything I know about assessment I learned from the best in the field, so I thank these numerous mentors and friends.

I appreciate the teachers who allowed peeks into their classrooms and whose students' remarkable work brings life to the activities in Section 4. Thanks especially to Lana Wostal for being so receptive and responsive.

Thanks to Bill Varner, my editor, who shared my vision for both the elementary title and this book for middle school teachers. Also, there's not a nicer group of people around than the editorial, production, and publicity teams at Stenhouse.

Jeff Anderson provided frequent (and humorous) encouragement, and Carol Bedard, while working with me on another project, never failed to check how I was doing on this one.

And importantly, thanks to John W. Jones, who has supported my work on this book (even before the ink was dry on the last one).

Introduction

By middle school, students are experienced test takers. Familiar with the drill, students know that on test day, they should be well rested, must eat breakfast, should dress comfortably, need sharpened number 2 pencils, and must get to school early or, at least, on time. During the test, they know to read the directions, record their answers in test booklets, and keep their eyes on their own paper.

These have become standard test-taking customs.

But not all advice about preparing to take a test is as straightforward. Think about all the mixed messages students have encountered as they have become experienced test takers:

- Skip questions you don't know and come back to them.
- Don't skip questions because you'll get off track in your answer booklet.

- Work slowly to avoid making a silly mistake.
- Work steadily to avoid overthinking things.

- Get up and sharpen your pencil during the test to give your brain a short break.
- Don't get up to sharpen your pencil during the test because it is distracting; bring extra pencils.

And let's not forget the myriad tips about how to read while taking a test:

- Read the questions first, then the passage.
- Read the passage first, then the questions.
- Read the title first.
- Study the pictures first.
- Read the subheadings first.

These go on and on.

Why? Because tests are serious business—very serious—and the stakes are high for students to perform well on tests.

Today more than ever, there is a great deal of bustling and upheaval over tests, which gives way to the dissemination of all kinds of lore. But do students who sharpen their pencils during the test do better or worse than students who don't? Not likely. Do students who notice the pictures before reading a passage do better than students who notice them after reading a passage? Probably not.

What matters is students' ability to make sense of the content on the test pages. And that very content is mysterious and confusing to teachers and students alike for a multitude of reasons. First, curriculum standards can be nebulous, intentionally or unintentionally. Another reason is that the lexicon of tests is not always a good match to classroom talk (Kohn 2000; Valencia and Villarreal 2003). Yet another reason is that the reading and thinking students are expected to do on tests is not always a good match with the reading work of classrooms. The list goes on.

Because testing has become pervasive on a national scale, a culture of panic is palpable in many, many school districts around the country. All states must select or create tests that are aligned with curriculum standards, students are tested frequently in core subjects, and states use the results of the tests to determine whether students are making adequate yearly progress. These tests are deemed high stakes because the scores also factor into decisions about students' grade-level advancement. Such pressure has led to a practice termed "teaching to the test," a departure from authentic reading instruction in favor of skill-based worksheets that are intended to help students creep toward a passing score (Firestone, Schorr, and Monfils 2004).

Yet reading teachers know that a steady regimen of test practice does not foster good reading habits and a lifelong love of reading in their students. Reading teachers know that school-mandated benchmarks and daily worksheet practice cause students to loathe reading and tests. It's no wonder that adolescent literacy advocates are pointing to tests as a contributor to the growing problem of aliteracy, which means that our middle school students *can read* but that they *aren't reading*. Tests are believed to crowd out more meaningful reading instruction and time spent truly engaged with texts, and the result is that once-avid readers in elementary school are becoming nonreaders in middle

"After 20 years of schooling, your aptitude test shows that you're skilled at just one thing - taking tests."

school, especially true of boys (Smith and Wilhelm 2002). Kelly Gallagher (2009) explains and explores the problem in his book *Readicide*, a term he defines as the systematic killing of the love of reading, often exacerbated by the inane, mind-numbing practices found in schools. Are we currently valuing the development of good test takers over the development of lifelong readers?

Reading teachers ultimately are finding themselves in a no-win situation: (1) they want their students to feel successful, but success is defined as a number on a score report; (2) they are not experts on testing, and they do not know where to turn for information about how reading standards are interpreted and assessed; and (3) they teach in a district where the philosophy is to "prepare" students with repeated testing practice, which often reinforces students' lack of understanding of tests and reading skills rather than increases their understanding.

Purpose of the Book

The reality is that the field of education is overwrought with well-meaning efforts to reframe curriculum standards so that they make more sense, are more teachable, are narrower and deeper in focus, and ultimately make students wiser. But the hang-up is that no one has figured out a way to satisfy the stakeholders in the educational enterprise with a more efficient means of reporting on students' learning than standardized assessments. As a result, students need opportunities to learn about these assessments. Teachers recognize that ignoring the reality of testing is a disservice to their students, yet they want to find ways to prepare their students without sacrificing high-quality teaching and learning. More and more sources and resources are coming into print that chronicle teachers' struggles and successes with rolling up their sleeves and constructing knowledge alongside their students about these unique sources of print called standardized tests, without having to give up their integrity in the process (Fuhrken and Roser 2010; Conrad et al. 2008; Greene and Melton 2007).

Teachers need better access to information about tests. Certainly the facets of test making are well documented (see, for instance, Downing and Haladyna's *Handbook of Test Development* [2006]), and state departments make their assessments as transparent as possible, which is why they release tests for teachers to study and use. But more often than not, the information about reading tests that is available to teachers is not packaged in a compact, ready-to-use, easy-to-understand form. If teachers knew more about how reading tests are made, how standards are interpreted and assessed, and how students can apply their knowledge of reading to the items that appear on reading tests, then teachers could spend much less time trying to figure out these tests and could feel less like servants to the dictates of their state assessment.

Making short work of informing teachers about what they need to know about reading assessments in order to prepare their students means giving back to teachers the instructional time that is often wasted on test practice instead of valuable reading instruction. It's really this simple: The more teachers know about the content of reading tests and the strategies students can use to access test items, the quicker they can deliver that information to their students, not in the form of worksheets, but through focused test preparation that involves rich, lively, engaging reading and thoughtful, meaning-making experiences with their peers. How freeing.

About the Author

I have helped write reading tests—lots of them. This is rather ironic, because I remember as a youngster reading dreadfully boring passages and wondering, with furrowed brow, "Who writes this stuff?" I had no idea that one day I would. I somewhat lucked into the profession, working as a freelance writer for a test publisher while teaching and attending graduate school. Now, more than fifteen years later, I have served as a reading content specialist for several test publishers and have contributed to the development of many state assessments— including those of California, Georgia, Mississippi, Texas, and Virginia—and have had a voice in state program transitions, such as Texas's STAAR and the Common Core State Standards.

In the process, I worked with hundreds of teachers who were asked by their state departments to review the tests that I helped write. Those meetings were fascinating, because there was so much information gathering and information sharing happening at once. The reading specialists from the state departments and test publishers were interested in hearing the wisdom of the teachers who were teaching the very content that was being assessed on a state's test. The teachers took the opportunity to ask the burning questions they had about the assessment, and oftentimes, the information that was shared influenced their perspective and instructional practices. Countless times, I heard teachers say, "I wish I had known that." I came to realize that if teachers knew more about the construction and content of a reading test, they wouldn't be wasting their time or their students' time by having to take stabs at how to best prepare their students. Those conversations with teachers inspired this book.

Organization of the Book

The book is divided into four sections.

Section 1, "Building Understandings About Tests," consists of two chapters that explore helping students gain test know-how. Chapter 1 tackles the language of tests and offers an effective strategy for collecting students' deepening knowledge of a reading test's lexicon. Chapter 2 offers guidelines and principles that can help students become savvy test takers.

Section 2, "Exploring Strategies for Reading Tests," takes a thorough look at the content of test items for the most commonly assessed reading standards. This section is not designed around any particular state assessment. The truth is, reading is reading, no matter where students live! That is, although state tests might look different on the surface, the skills needed to master any reading assessment are essentially the same. Section 2 divides those reading standards into strands and provides sample items and strategic approaches to answering those items. Before delving into this section, it is important to read the passage titled "The Gym Class ~~Nobody~~ Somebody" on pages 25–26. The discussions are based on items written for this passage.

Section 3, "Putting Strategies to Work," offers several passages and items that are similar to those featured on most state reading assessments for the middle school grades. Tips in the margin are included as scaffolding as students learn to think through the common item types and apply the strategies explored in Section 2.

Section 4, "Demonstrating Understandings with Reading Activities," provides a multitude of resources—activities that relate to specific reading standards as well as helpful lists and books that can be incorporated easily into teachers' reading work with students.

Building Understandings About Tests

It can be painful for a teacher to watch a student taking a test, especially when the student chews off half of his or her eraser in the process. Sometimes the content of the test puzzles a student and causes him or her to fret and shuffle and stare off into the distance. Sometimes it's the way the test "communicates"—or doesn't communicate!—to the test taker that interferes with a test taker's ability to show what he or she knows by selecting a "correct" idea.

The purpose of the two chapters in this section is to build understandings about tests. Chapter 1 is a guide for helping students build a test vocabulary—the language and genre-specific terms that allow students to navigate reading tests more efficiently and easily. Chapter 2 is a guide for helping students build what I call "test savvy"—information about test design, or the lay of the land, as well as tips for developing a plan as a confident and capable test taker. Each chapter provides mini-lessons for confirming students' understandings and bringing about new understandings of tests.

The following list of terminology is provided so that readers can consult it as needed while working through this section as well as the remainder of the book. An example test item follows the list to help explain some of the terms.

Terminology

Item: A test question with its answer choices. The terms *item* and *question* are interchangeable. The sample items presented throughout the book are multiple-choice items with four answer choices. Another common type is the constructed-response item (also called a *short-response item*, an *open-ended item*, or an *essay question*).

7

Stem: The beginning part of an item, which presents the task or problem. A *closed* stem ends with a question mark and is a complete thought. An *open* stem uses no punctuation at the end or uses a dash; the stem and the correct answer together form a complete thought.

Options: The answer choices. The terms *options* and *answer choices* are interchangeable.

Correct answer: The one option that is clearly defensible as correct in a multiple-choice item.

Distractors: The options that are incorrect in a multiple-choice item; also referred to as *wrong options*. (Sometimes spelled *distracters*.)

Passage: The text that test takers read prior to and while answering an item set. (There are many possible types/genres of texts.)

Standard: The core skill or criterion to which an item is written. Also called *objective, goal, expectation*, and *skill*.

Field test items: Items that collect data about students' performance but that do not count toward students' scores; they are often embedded in an *operational form* (see next term).

Operational form: The test form that purports to measure students' knowledge of curriculum standards and is the basis of students' scores. Also called a *live administration*.

Reporting category: A category within which standards are grouped for the purpose of reporting students' scores.

Examples

Standard: Analyze character traits.

In paragraph 1, how does the farmer feel?   ← *closed stem*

Options for closed-stem items usually begin with capital letters.
↓

distractors   A Puzzled
               B Confident
               C Eager

correct answer → D Angry

In paragraph 1, the farmer feels—   ← *open stem*

Options for open-stem items usually do not use capital letters.
↓
A puzzled
B confident
C eager
D angry ← *Options that are not complete sentences on their own may not have end punctuation; some assessments use end punctuation if the stem and the option together form a complete sentence.*

Chapter 1

Helping Students Build a Test Vocabulary

Sometimes my sister calls me when my middle school nephew's homework has her baffled. Often it has been too many years since she has had to call up some kind of language arts–related knowledge. "Remind me what hyperbole is," she might say.

Other times she'll be shut out of a conversation by today's methods of instruction.

> **Sister:** What did you do today, Kristopher?
> **Nephew:** Socratic circles.
> **Sister:** Oh. (*Long pause.*) That's nice.

Such is the language of reading classrooms. *Fix-up strategies. Inferences. Self-selected reading. Concept maps. Anticipation guides. Think-alouds. Talking drawings. Literature circles. I-Search. Exit tickets.* Parents, being outsiders to the goings-on in the reading classrooms, are often left unable to assist in homework situations—or even ask about their children's day—simply because they're not privy to that lexicon.

The same is true about standardized assessments for some students. Veteran middle school teacher Donna Santman (2002) considers the language of assessments to be a "quirky code" (209). True, assessments can sometimes communicate ideas in ways that students must find odd, likely due to a number of conventions of efficiency. For example, multiple-choice items are written tightly, with as few words as possible to communicate an idea. Most assessment specialists would say that word-cutting measures benefit the test taker by maintaining appropriate reading loads, potentially reducing reading fatigue. Likely

9

an equally important reason is almost entirely economical—more words across many pages means more paper and ink and increased printing costs. What this all means is that some multiple-choice questions are constructed with so few words, so tautly, so cryptically, that students cannot make sense of what is being asked. For some students, just a few more words might make the difference between sense and nonsense.

Reading tests have many ways of "discussing" the same idea. Conclusions, inferences, interpretations. Those are all just newfangled ways of saying "reading between the lines," which is what critical thinking was called when I was learning to read.

Because the ways in which reading is presented on assessments is less simple these days—it is more encoded and exceedingly proper (Calkins, Montgomery, and Santman, 1998)—students need opportunities to gain access to the language of tests; otherwise they'll have a limited ability to demonstrate what they know (Kohn 2000; Valencia and Villarreal 2003).

When a gulf exists between how reading skills and strategies are taught and understood in the classroom and how students are expected to apply those skills and strategies on a reading test, test items become riddles for students and they spent much of their time perplexed over why test language sounds very different from classroom talk. Familiarity with test-speak is critical for helping students gain access to the tasks and demands of test items.

An Example of When Tests and Classrooms Misalign

In the classroom, while discussing a narrative, teachers and students might address a story's problem as follows:

What is the main character's problem in this story?
What problem is Sarah facing?
What is the problem that Luis is trying to solve?

Yet on a standardized assessment, an item about story problem might be posed in a number of ways:

What is the conflict of the story?
How does the author build tension when the story opens?
What central conflict must Sarah overcome?
What challenging situation must Luis work to resolve?
How does the setting contribute to the main character's dilemma?

A reading standard phrased "identify a story's problem" provides no indication that a student might be expected to think about story problem under various names. Are middle schoolers likely to connect the word *problem* to its array of synonyms? Probably, mostly because the words *conflict, tension,* and *dilemma* likely exist in a middle school student's everyday speaking vocabulary, but not necessarily because the synonyms were introduced in the reading classroom as part of a discussion of story problem.

It's when the test's vocabulary is outside of the reading classroom's lexicon and beyond a student's natural speaking/listening/reading vocabularies that the disconnect presents serious issues for students. Building a common test vocabulary as part of daily reading instruction can help close the gap between classroom talk and test talk.

Introducing Students to Specialized Vocabularies

If you want students to understand the concept of a specialized vocabulary, just show them a short clip of any business presentation (from YouTube, perhaps) made by an MBA. Students might notice that an MBA often speaks in acronyms, expecting everyone in the room to be familiar with them. Or you might call a technology help desk. Students might notice that the "help" person often assumes the caller has the same amount of technical knowledge as he or she does.

Students who conceptualize tests as employing a specialized vocabulary can become more attuned to the language of standardized tests. Their antennas will perk up when they read test items. They will be able to attach new learning to old learning and create file cabinets in their brains about what skills go with particular kinds of vocabulary. They will view themselves as good readers, as readers who have read widely and discussed broadly, as literate folks who can join others in conversations about what they are reading—the genres, the elements and techniques, the perspectives and views, and their connections with other authors. They will be able to "converse" with reading tests.

MINI-LESSON Every Subject Has a Language

Provide students with highlighters and copies of recently released tests in a number of subject areas other than reading, such as science and math. Ask students to work in groups to highlight in each item at least one specialized word that a test taker must know in order to begin to make sense of the item. Have students use markers to transfer their examples of specialized vocabulary to chart paper labeled appropriately (for example, "Science Vocabulary"). Ask students to discuss why these words are important to know.

Repeat the process using a reading test form. Model by drawing attention to an item about main idea, pointing out that test takers must know that a main idea refers to the most important idea or a major idea in a text rather than a minor detail. Allow students to work in pairs to collect reading test language and discuss them as a class.

MINI-LESSON Same Thing, Different Words

Prepare in advance by reviewing several released tests in reading from many states. (These can be found on official Web sites of states' departments of education.) Find items that essentially ask about the same skill but in different ways. For example, story problem might be asked about using the word *problem, conflict, dilemma,* or *trouble.* Copy and cut out several examples of the same skill to create a set. Make four sets.

Divide students into four groups. Distribute one set of test items, chart paper, and tape to each group. Ask students to read the items and name a category the items belong to, using the story problem example above as a model.

When groups are finished working, share across groups and discuss that reading tests ask about reading concepts in a variety of ways.

Building Students' Test Vocabularies

Once students become aware that test makers expect students to know various terms, they can begin to notice and discuss these terms during their everyday reading activities. They can begin to determine the breadth and depth of learning that they need to exhibit on test day. They can begin to recognize reading terms, define them, search for and obtain memorable examples of them, and relate them to other terms and aspects of reading. Teachers can help students collect these observations by using various graphic organizers to help students group their knowledge to specific reading subskills. Over time and with wide reading of texts, students can add to their understandings. Following are examples of the kind of information students may need to collect in order to demonstrate their knowledge of reading subskills on standardized tests.

✓ *Persuasive Writing Terms*

Figure 1.1 is essentially a word wall about persuasive writing terms. When it is exhibited in the classroom, students can refer to this display and adopt the language of analyzing persuasive texts that will likely appear on assessments.

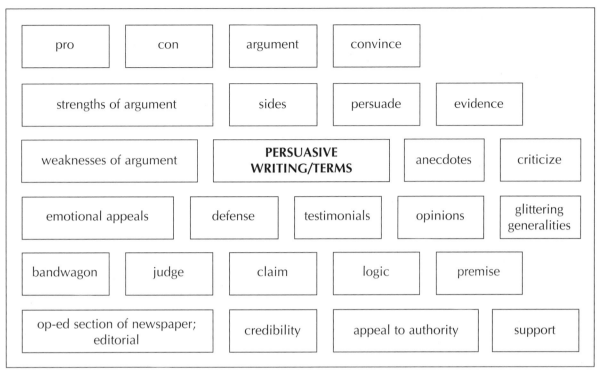

FIGURE 1.1
Sample Word Wall of Persuasive Writing Terms

✓ *Author's Purpose and Genre*

Aren't there only three main purposes for writing: to entertain, to inform, and to persuade? Not according to most reading tests. As students collect these "variations," they might also think about the genres to which these "purpose words" belong. Often the lines are blurred, which makes for interesting classroom discussion and deeper analysis of text. Figure 1.2 is a basic Venn diagram with a few purpose words filled in, based on the genre. Below the diagram are

FIGURE 1.2
Sample Venn Diagram for
Organizing Purpose Words

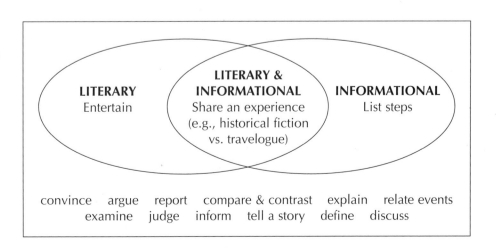

"purpose words" that commonly appear on assessments; students could place these purpose words within the diagram. Have students discuss and find examples to support whether the purpose word belongs only to one genre or both.

✓ *Author's Organization*

In Figure 1.3, the left column shows some of the patterns that students might be responsible for knowing by name, and the right column offers space for students to add text examples as they find them.

FIGURE 1.3
Common Author's
Organization Terms and
Examples

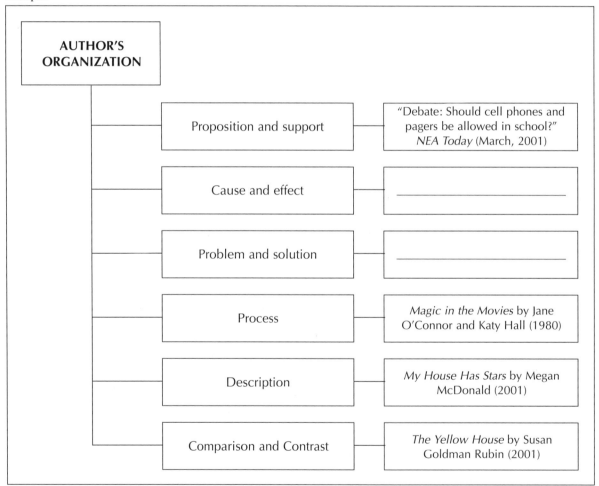

AUTHOR'S ORGANIZATION	
Proposition and support	"Debate: Should cell phones and pagers be allowed in school?" *NEA Today* (March, 2001)
Cause and effect	_____
Problem and solution	_____
Process	*Magic in the Movies* by Jane O'Connor and Katy Hall (1980)
Description	*My House Has Stars* by Megan McDonald (2001)
Comparison and Contrast	*The Yellow House* by Susan Goldman Rubin (2001)

More Ideas for Collecting Reading Knowledge

1. Use a jigsaw approach to helping students dig deeply into fiction types (e.g., realistic fiction, folktale, myth, fantasy, historical fiction). After

each group of students explores definitions, descriptions, characteristics, and examples of a particular fiction type, allow these now-experts to present their findings.

2. Discuss common approaches for presenting information in nonfiction texts. Collect examples of stylistic techniques, such as beginning with a shocking fact, sharing an anecdote, making a joke, and asking rhetorical questions. Collect examples of nonfiction features, such as subheadings and sidebars. Call them by name so that students will be prepared for identifying and analyzing these same techniques and features on assessments.

3. Students are asked on tests to interpret information for a number of reading subskills: cause-effect, chronology, conclusion/inference, fact/opinion, and so forth. For cause-effect items, students might be asked about a *result* or *outcome*, so they need to be familiar with these terms as synonyms for *effect*. Gather terms that are signals for interpretations as students build their test vocabularies. See Chapter 8 (in Section 2) for samples of item stems in order to collect a variety of terms.

More Ideas for Collecting Reading Test Knowledge

1. Mark out essential reading terms in a set of reading items. For instance, change the item "What is the main idea of paragraph 9?" to "What is the _____ of paragraph 9?" (Some terms for marking out include *detail, character, point of view, organization, purpose,* and *conclude.*) Ask students to read the passage and use the answer choices of the items to infer the reading-related term that has been marked out. Then have students check their guesses. Discuss the clues in the item that helped students determine the missing term.

2. Take a set of reading items and separate the item stems from the answer choices. Ask students to match them up. Allow students to discuss the items that were easy to match up and those that required more thinking. Have students talk about the connections they make between how certain kinds of questions are posed and how certain kinds of answers are worded.

3. Using an item set for one passage from a released test, present students with only the correct answers to the questions. Then ask students to work in groups to formulate a question for each answer. When students have finished working, allow groups to share with the class the questions they developed for each correct answer. Discuss how the groups' questions are alike and different. Then share the actual stem from the released test. Further discuss the groups' question in relation to the real

test question. Help students notice important features of item construction and how reading terms are embedded in items as clues.

When students are steeped in the language of tests, they are less likely to encounter terms or labels for concepts that will leave them stymied. Knowing the lexicon makes students "insiders" and less vulnerable to feeling like tests are something that happens to them rather than something that they command. Furthermore, when students are in the know about test tasks and demands and understand what is being asked of them, their responses—and ultimately their test scores—more accurately reflect their abilities and knowledge in reading.

Chapter 2

Helping Students Become Test Savvy

I grew up thinking that there were two kinds of test takers: those who tested well and those who didn't. I considered myself in the second category. I accepted my fate, thinking that testing well was a natural gift and I'd never be able to develop the ability.

It's not that I didn't do well on tests, actually. But there were always a few test items that I wanted to argue with. True-false questions were a nightmare because I could convince myself that a statement was both true *and* false. For multiple-choice questions, I'd find at least two options that were correct—at least in my mind.

My teachers often tried to make me feel better by calling me a divergent thinker.

The truth, more likely, is that I was so busy arguing with the test that I never let the test teach me anything. Good test takers know about tests. They know not to be seduced by shades of truth. They can feel for the rhythm of the item. They know how to apply what they know with laser-like precision. The correct answers practically appear in neon.

I once read about the sheer number of tests that students will encounter before they graduate high school. I should have made note of that source. I suppose I didn't because I was struck by two things: (1) the number was so shocking, and (2) I realized that in all my years of schooling, I had never learned to be more test savvy. If students will be subjected to lots of tests during their lifetimes, then why aren't we doing more to talk about tests, explore them, expose them, and get smarter about them?

That's what this chapter is about: helping students who have yet to show themselves as good test takers to cross over to the other side.

Increasing Students' Knowledge of Item Construction

Multiple-choice items are hard to mistake. Even young students learn quickly that multiple-choice items have a few features that remain consistent from one to another: a concisely worded stem along with several possible answers, all of which are concisely worded as well. Because test takers can expect items to look this way, they do not have to waste a lot of brainpower trying to figure out an item's basic structure.

Multiple-choice items tend to "sound" a certain way as well. When items are constructed, the item writers do not simply write anything they want, any way they want. They follow guidelines that are provided by the test publisher, and these guidelines are quite similar regardless of the type or purpose of a test. Just search the Internet for "item writing guidelines" or grab any book about the test development process and you'll find that whether it's a reading test, a nursing certification test, or a college entrance exam, there are agreed-upon ways to construct multiple-choice items. That's a good thing—especially since students will be taking all kinds of tests during their lifetimes.

Knowing how items are constructed can help students a great deal as test takers. Figure 2.1 shows some of the most common guidelines for constructing multiple-choice items as well as how sample items have been appropriately revised. Teachers can keep the guidelines in mind during their discussions with students about tests, mostly because students' scores can suffer when they develop their own ideas and theories about test items that are not true.

MINI-LESSON In the Test Maker's Shoes

Before discussing item guidelines with the class, allow students to take a stab at item writing. Designate a particular text (say, three paragraphs or more) and ask each student to construct one multiple-choice test item. Encourage students to write the item stem, the correct answer, and at least one wrong option.

Present and discuss the item guidelines that you think are important for students to understand.

In small groups, have students review their items and make appropriate edits based on each of the principles about item construction they learn.

If desired, have students work in groups to construct several more items that take into account the item guidelines presented to them.

Options should not be visually appealing or distracting because of length or specificity.

Original	**Revised**
In paragraph 1, how does the farmer feel?	In paragraph 1, how does the farmer feel?
A Puzzled	A Puzzled by the animals' behavior
B Angry about the condition of the land	B Angry about the condition of the land

---

Options should not be visually appealing or distracting because of emphasis.

Original	**Revised**
In paragraph 1, how does the farmer feel?	In paragraph 1, how does the farmer feel?
A Puzzled	A Puzzled
B Angry and hopeless	B Angry

Options should not be imbalanced in terms of positives and negatives.

Original		**Revised**	
In paragraph 1, how does the farmer feel?		In paragraph 1, how does the farmer feel?	
A Satisfied	(+)	A Angry	(–)
B Confident	(+)	B Confident	(+)
C Eager	(+)	C Eager	(+)
D Cowardly	(–)	D Cowardly	(–)

Options should not use vocabulary that is above grade level.

Original	**Revised**
In paragraph 1, how does the farmer feel?	In paragraph 1, how does the farmer feel?
A Puzzled	A Puzzled
B Vexed	B Angry

Options should not be figurative or idiomatic in meaning.

Original	**Revised**
In paragraph 1, how does the farmer feel?	In paragraph 1, how does the farmer feel?
A Puzzled	A Puzzled
B Madder than a hornet	B Angry

FIGURE 2.1
Sample Test Item Guidelines *(continued on next page)*

Options should not have multiple interpretations.

Original	**Revised**
In paragraph 1, how does the farmer feel?	In paragraph 1, how does the farmer feel?
A Proud (pleased? or conceited?)	A Pleased
B Surprised (amazed? or shocked?)	B Amazed
C Anxious (eager? or nervous?)	C Eager
D Thoughtful (caring? or mindful?)	D Caring

Options should not express the same idea with different words.

Original	**Revised**
Why does the farmer stare at the sky for two days?	Why does the farmer stare at the sky for two days?
A He hopes the skies will change soon. (correct answer)	A He has nothing else to do. (now incorrect)
B He is looking for a sign of rain. (correct answer)	B He is looking for a sign of rain. (now the only correct answer)

Item stems should not contain a clue about the correct answer.

Original	**Revised**
Which detail shows that the farmer is hopeful?	Which detail shows that the farmer is hopeful?
A He hopes it will rain.	A He expects rain to fall eventually.

Items should not provide clues to other items or assess the same idea.

This Item Clues This One →	**← This Item Clues This One**
Why does the hopeful farmer "stare at the sky for two days"?	Which idea shows that the farmer is hopeful?
A He is looking for a sign of rain.	A He stares at the sky for two days.

FIGURE 2.1
Sample Test Item Guidelines *(continued)*

Items have only one job to do, which is to allow students to demonstrate what they know. Item guidelines help ensure that students can focus their attention on what the item asks (the reading content) rather than how the item asks it (the construction). It makes sense to introduce students to the principles of good test construction so that they become savvier about how test items look and sound. When they themselves don a test maker's hat and give item writing a try, they have the potential to become better test takers—better test "thinkers"—as a result.

Bone Up on a Test's Tasks

Smart preparation for a test involves discussions about assessment. Students may not be sufficiently prepared for a reading assessment simply because they read well and widely over the course of a year. Standards today require much more focused instruction, and assessments today—because of the many variations they invoke when asking test takers about reading skills—require teachers and students to devote some attention to advance preparation for specific test tasks. Teachers shouldn't be so fearful of "teaching to the test" criticisms that they swing their instructional practices to the far end of the continuum. If they do, students may be totally off-put when assessment week arrives in the spring. After all, even students who have experience with taking tests can feel displaced come test day. Students can become confounded if they have been in a classroom for a year in which the teacher invites and accepts a variety of responses from students' discussions of literature, but then on test day, that same teacher tells students that they must pick only one answer—the "correct" one.

Students can feel more confident if they have researched what to expect on an upcoming assessment. (Imagine taking the GRE without having practiced reasoning out analogies!) Test anxiety can heighten when students come across content that they do not expect and when they have not developed strategies for thinking through that content. Knowing what they will be required to do when they open the test booklet and with each turn of the test page helps provide them with the confidence they will need to demonstrate their competence in reading.

MINI-LESSON Let Me Get to Know You, Test

Have students brainstorm questions they have about an upcoming assessment and then use resources (such as released test items, sample forms, or blueprints) and your state education department's Web site to determine the answers. Some questions might be the following:

- How many passages might I have to read?
- What types of items (multiple-choice, open-ended, essay) are required?
- What are the genres/types of passages I might have to read? Will some passages be paired?
- What questions seem harder and will require more time and thought? (Questions that ask about inferences? Questions about paired passages?)
- What features (subtitles, visuals) are provided that will help me as a reader?

- What features or clues about the items are provided by the test? (Are vocabulary words underlined? Do a few of or a lot of the questions provide paragraph references?)

As students develop and then research their questions, use their findings to discuss these and other important test issues.

MINI-LESSON   My Personal Plan

Students who have a plan of attack, so to speak, are likely to approach the test with more confidence about their ability to read and to do a good job of communicating that knowledge as they answer the test's items.

Tell students that they will be responsible for developing their own reading plan as test takers. The goal is to get students talking about and conscious of the strategies they intend to use as they encounter test demands.

Begin by having students brainstorm some scenarios that they have faced or might face as test takers. Here are some possible questions:

- What should I do when I first see a passage? (Read the title; get information from text features, such as photographs, maps, and charts.)
- What should I do when I get to a long passage or a hard passage? (Stop every few paragraphs to summarize; adjust reading rate; circle key words.)
- What strategies that I use as an everyday reader will work well as a reader of test materials? (Visualizing; rereading; predicting; using prior knowledge.)

Refer to classroom artifacts (such as anchor charts) that speak to the students' questions as appropriate.

Decide how students will capture their thinking in this exercise. For example, students could work as a class to come up with their "Top Ten" smart test-taking tips, make illustrated crib sheets, and/or write and perform a skit that compares the experiences of an unprepared test taker to those of a smart test taker.

When students try their hands at the art and science of item writing, and when they read, strategize, and discuss test tasks, they become better prepared to demonstrate what they know about reading. When teachers help students think about and think through test formats and features (especially particular types of test items), teachers are strengthening students' skill at negotiating the many ideas that confront them within the pages of a test booklet, all the while building their confidence and capabilities as test takers.

Exploring Strategies for Reading Tests

This section is designed with two questions in mind:

1. What is tested on most middle school reading assessments?
2. What strategies can students use to answer those reading items?

The truth is that reading tests are mostly the same. No matter how reading curriculum standards and test objectives are worded, students essentially encounter the same types of reading items for the same types of reading standards.

To make exploring the test content and reading strategies manageable, more than thirty of the most commonly assessed reading standards have been grouped in this book into six strands. Each chapter in Section 2 is devoted to one of these strands: Vocabulary Development, Important Ideas, Literary Elements, Literary Techniques, Interpretations, and Text Matters. Sample items and strategic approaches for answering those items are presented. These strategies are designed to be used individually or in combination. Oftentimes, more strategies are offered than students need, but the intent is to be as comprehensive as possible when presenting strategies that work. After all, students are empowered when they have many strategies and tools available to them and have learned when and how to apply them. Furthermore, although all the sample items are written in a multiple-choice format, students can use the strategies offered for other formats as well, such as with open-ended items. And for ease of reading, all the options in the sample items appear as ABCD, even though the custom for actual test items is to follow an alternating pattern of ABCD and FGHJ.

The passage that follows, "The Gym Class ~~Nobody~~ Somebody," represents a typical middle school test passage and is the basis of the sample items and discussions about the strategies throughout Section 2, so read this passage first and consult it as needed while working through the chapters in this section.

Sample Passage

The Gym Class ~~Nobody~~ Somebody

By Jake Kinnett

1   The Texas heat is the enemy. Sweat on my forehead rushes like a river to my eyes. Rubbing them doesn't lessen the stinging, but I cannot resist. Every day is the same in my eighth-grade gym class. I stand, unnoticed, in right field. I take off my baseball glove because I know I won't need it. I wait for class to be over the way a prisoner waits to be released. I wind the dial of my watch and tap on it, thinking the second hand has stopped moving.

2   But on this particular day, with 3 minutes and 42 seconds remaining, something happens that has never happened before. There is a fly ball heading my way and nobody else is near. At first I think that I am seeing things. Because the sun punishes us with blinding rays, it is quite possible that I am being deceived. It takes only the shouts of my teammates to know that I am not <u>delusional</u>. "Get under it, Jake," someone commands. "Don't be scared of it," someone else hollers. A baseball is indeed heading toward me— the too-tall, chubby, clumsy kid who, while respected on campus for guitar playing, is lost on the sports field.

3   And then the ball pauses in midair while I am transported back to the fourth grade. Setting: Playground. "I'm open," I yell at my football team's quarterback, Paul Herrera. But every quarterback knows not to throw the ball to the person who is consistently picked last, who is allowed to play only because the teacher is watching. So I know it is <u>improbable</u> that my hands will touch that ball. Sure enough, Paul tries desperately to <u>catch</u> the eye of another teammate. But they are all heavily guarded. No one ever guards me. The nearest opponent is three city blocks away.

4   Paul takes one more look down the field. I can hear Paul's thought: *If Hector or Mike has the slightest opportunity to receive this pass, I'll throw it to one of them rather than waste the play on Jake.* I know I have to persuade him otherwise. So I lock eyes with him. And I yell, louder this time, "I'm open." *Come on. Throw it to me,* I <u>implore</u> in my head.

5   That's when Paul does the unthinkable. He actually tosses the football directly, perfectly, gingerly to me. I do what I have seen my classmates do countless times before, but which I have never been given the opportunity on the school playground to do: I stick out my hands, grasp the ball, and pull it to my chest. I glance at Paul, and neither he nor I can believe I have caught it. Thirty yards separate me from a touchdown. So I run—fast. I travel nearly twenty yards before the others—stunned that I, Jake Hartman, have possession of the ball—can make their way to me. I have fewer than five yards to go when Terry, the steamroller, beelines it for me, grabs a fistful of shirt, and yanks. I hit the ground hard. The ball? It slips from my hands as though they were buttered. The shouts from my peers "Fumble. He fumbled!" redden my face and mock me the rest of the day.

6   Then the words "You've got this one, Jake" take me from football back to baseball. Again, I stick out my hands, ready to accept the ball that the bat was intent on delivering to me. It lands with a thud—in my ungloved hands—and it stays put. There is no way I can mess up this moment. There's no such thing as a fumble in baseball.

7   "Way to go, Jake" is the first cheer I hear. There are others—lots of them. In fact, I barely hear the coach's whistle, signaling the game is over.

8   As we head to the locker room, I keep admiring that baseball in my still-stinging hands. When I go to place it in the equipment locker, I run into Coach Wilson. "Nice catch," he says.

9   I look down at the mound in the metal ball basket. Then I ask, "Mind if I keep this one, Coach?" I figure one fewer ball in the equipment locker won't matter. But that ball does matter to me. A lot.

10   "No problem," he says, flashing a knowing smile and patting me on the back. I smile, too, pocketing my ball proudly.

11   For the rest of the day, my gloveless catch is big news. In math class, instead of doing their work, the guys entertain some girls by recounting the moment in a dramatic sportscaster's voice.

12   Now, this is the part of the story where I wish I could tell you that my status took roots. The truth is that the next day, when teams were being picked, I stood there, the best guitar player around, and was chosen—last. But having a desire to improve my ranking, I put on my glove, which covered up my watch, and I hustled to right field. Not even the intense Texas sun could keep me from watching the sky for a ball heading my way.

Chapter 3

Vocabulary Development

This chapter presents information about the most common types of items used to assess vocabulary on state assessments. These include context clues, prefixes and suffixes, roots, multiple-meaning words, and connotation. The following are examples, not particular to any state, of reading standards for vocabulary development. Students are expected to do the following:

- Use *context clues* to derive the meaning of unfamiliar words
- Apply knowledge of word parts such as *prefixes, suffixes,* and *derivational endings* to recognize words
- Use *root words* to determine word meaning
- Recognize which meaning of a *multiple-meaning word* applies to a word's use within a passage
- Identify the *connotation* of familiar words

Basic Strategies for Vocabulary Items

The following basic strategies are good starting points for teachers to share with students as they work together to make sense of reading test items about vocabulary. Later in this chapter, strategies that are specific to certain types of vocabulary items are explored.

✓ *Don't panic when encountering a vocabulary item that tests an unknown word.*

Encountering a word that students do not know is often the frightening part of a vocabulary item on an assessment. Even the most fearless readers can freeze when they come across a word they do not know. What students need to know is that reading items testing vocabulary *intentionally* focus on words that are likely *unfamiliar* to them so that they can use their reading strategies to determine the meanings of unknown words. Therefore, students should be told explicitly that they are not expected to know the meanings of the vocabulary words—they are expected to figure out the meanings.

✓ *Recognize the item type and locate important information in the item.*

Savvy test takers pay attention to the directions and cues that are provided in items. For most vocabulary items, a word or phrase is selected from the passage, and students are asked to uncover its meaning. Usually the item is presented in a straightforward manner, as in, "What does <u>tested word</u> mean in paragraph X?" Most assessments underline or use quotation marks to set off the tested word in the stem. The tested word may be underlined in the passage so that students can locate it easily; however, the publishers/authors of previously published passages may not permit doing so. Students might need practice with recognizing the kind of information in an item that is intended to be helpful to them.

✓ *Return to the passage and reread beyond the targeted sentence and paragraph.*

Students will *not* have all the information they need in the item stem and answer choices for most types of vocabulary items; that is why a paragraph reference appears in most vocabulary items. Passage references are big hints that rereading is necessary to arrive at the correct answer.

Still, the paragraph reference in a context clue vocabulary item does not mean that the context clues appear in that paragraph! Clues are not always found in such close proximity to the tested words as the same sentence or the sentences immediately before or after. Sometimes clues can be found in the paragraphs before or after the paragraph in which the tested word appears. And on middle school assessments of reading, students may be expected to pick up on more subtle clues, such as the author's tone and sentence structure/syntax, in order to determine word meaning. Therefore, students may need practice with determining how to expand their search for context clues beyond the sentence and the paragraph in which the tested word appears.

Context Clues

In paragraph 4, the word <u>implore</u> means to—

A   question
B   practice
C   wonder
D   plead

Correct answer: D

Strategies

✓ *Locate important information in the item.*

The item stem tells students the following:

• What word is being tested (*implore*)
• Where the tested word is located (paragraph 4)

✓ *Return to the passage and reread beyond the targeted sentence and paragraph.*

At a minimum, students should reread paragraph 4 to search for context clues. If more clues are needed, they should expand their search.

✓ *Know a variety of context clues.*

Synonym clues are the easiest to detect, so students tend to favor this type of context clue. Students might need practice with using other types of clues, such as those in Figure 3.1.

In this item, descriptive clues are present, not synonym clues. Students have to put together a number of ideas:

• In paragraph 3, the author establishes that "every quarterback knows not to throw the ball to the person who is consistently picked last."
• In paragraph 4, Jake claims to know what the quarterback is thinking—that throwing the ball to Jake would be a wasted play; as a result, Jake knows he has to change the quarterback's mind ("I know I have to persuade him otherwise").

• Also in paragraph 4, Jake locks eyes with and yells again to the quarterback.

By using these descriptive clues, students should determine that Jake desperately wants the quarterback to throw the ball his way. To *implore* someone to do something means to *plead*. Option D is correct.

✓ *Use substitution.*

Substitution is a popular strategy for vocabulary items, probably because it is the easiest to use, but substitution should not be students' only strategy. Substitution as a sole or main strategy can lead students to believe that they need not look beyond the tested sentence for clues, and that one answer choice will make sense when substituted into the tested sentence while the three others will not.

FIGURE 3.1 **Types of Context Clues**

Synonym clue	In two short weeks, the physician's assistant had become <u>indispensable</u>. The new receptionist served an *essential* role in the front office *as well.*
Antonym clue	The art curator thought he had acquired an *original* work, *but* later he discovered that the painting was actually a <u>replica</u>.
Example clue	Although the dressmaker worked with *many textures of fabric,* <u>damask</u> was her least favorite.
Description clue	Martha is quite <u>studious</u>. *She reads her textbooks long after most people have gone to bed. On weekends, she frequents the library.*
Definition clue	My friend Dan has a bad case of <u>ophidiophobia</u>, or *fear of snakes*; he's even afraid of the snakes in science magazines!
Cause-effect clue	The house was so <u>deteriorated</u> that the city was forced to *tear it down.*

In this item, because the tested word and the answer choices are the same part of speech, students can substitute the answer choices into the tested sentence easily:

A *Come on. Throw it to me*, I <u>question</u> in my head.

B *Come on. Throw it to me*, I <u>practice</u> in my head.

C *Come on. Throw it to me*, I <u>wonder</u> in my head.

D *Come on. Throw it to me*, I <u>plead</u> in my head.

Stripped from the context of the passage, all of these sentences make a little sense. In other words, planting the answer choices in the tested sentence does not render three nonsense sentences and one that makes perfect sense. So, substitution alone will not lead students to the correct answer.

Students must combine this substitution strategy with their knowledge of the descriptive context clues they should have uncovered as they reread paragraphs 3 and 4. Doing so will help them confirm that Jake is trying intently to persuade the quarterback to throw the ball to him. His words are a plea. Option D is the correct answer.

✓ *Examine the sentence structure and tone.*

Students should examine the sentence in which the tested word appears to determine if there are syntactic or other clues that can help them. In this item, the tested sentence is "*Come on. Throw it to me*, I <u>implore</u> in my head." Students should recognize that the word *implore* is a verb and that Jake is saying in his head the words that appear in italics. Because a verb is an action, students need to think about *how* Jake is saying those words; they should consider Jake's tone as he says those words.

Because Jake says, "I yell, louder this time," there is urgency on Jake's part. Jake locks eyes with the quarterback because he doesn't want the quarterback to think he has any other option but to throw the ball to Jake. Jake is not "questioning," "practicing," or "wondering"—these options do not have meanings that adequately capture the gravity of the situation for Jake. Only option D, "plead," sufficiently represents Jake's mind-set.

Context Clues

Which words found in paragraph 2 help the reader know what <u>delusional</u> means?

A *has never happened before*
B *I am seeing things*
C *someone commands*
D *lost on the sports field*

Correct answer: B

Strategies

✓ *Recognize the item type.*
This item type measures students' ability to select the words in the passage that serve as context clues rather than identify the meaning of the tested word.

✓ *Locate important information in the item.*
The item tells students the following:

- What word is being tested (*delusional*)
- Where the tested word is located (paragraph 2)
- That the options are lifted directly from the passage (key words: *found in*; use of italics)

✓ *Return to the passage and reread beyond the targeted sentence and paragraph.*
Because students are being asked to determine which actual words from the passage serve as context clues, rereading only the tested sentence won't get students very far. The only way to determine the answer is to reread the paragraph to determine if the words presented in the options contribute to the meaning of the word *delusional*.

Furthermore, this item sets up students to think that only one context clue is present in the passage for the word *delusional*—because there can be only one right answer to any item! But there are at least two context clues in paragraph 2

that stand out. Students should find that the phrases *I am seeing things* and *I am being deceived* support the meaning of *delusional*. By considering these clues, students will likely determine that option B is the answer.

✓ *Construct try-out sentences, a form of substitution.*
Because students are asked to identify the clue that suggests the meaning of *delusional*, they cannot simply substitute the options into the tested sentence and expect the tested sentence to make sense. Sometimes, though, they can construct try-out sentences, a form of substitution that manipulates the options so that they make some sense:

A It takes only the shouts of my teammates for me to know that I am not <u>experiencing something that has never happened before</u>.
B It takes only the shouts of my teammates for me to know that I am not <u>seeing things</u>.
C It takes only the shouts of my teammates for me to know that I am not <u>hearing someone command</u>.
D It takes only the shouts of my teammates for me to know that I am not <u>lost on the sports field</u>.

This strategy is best employed when students already have a hunch about the correct answer (because they have used other strategies). That is, students who think that option B is the correct answer can quickly determine that try-out sentence B, "It takes only the shouts of my teammates to know that I am not <u>seeing things</u>," makes sense in the context of the passage. Jake knows that his teammates would not be shouting at him unless they wanted him to do something—catch the ball!

Options A, C, and D make little sense.

Prefixes and Suffixes

In paragraph 3, the word <u>improbable</u> means—

A   happening before
B   able to happen
C   likely to happen again
D   not likely to happen

Correct answer: D

Strategies

Note: The strategies shown here can be applied to *suffix* items that are structured similarly.

✓ *Locate important information in the item.*

The item stem tells students the following:

- What word is being tested (*improbable*)
- Where the tested word is located (paragraph 3)

✓ *Look for familiar word parts.*

When answering vocabulary items, students should first look for word parts they recognize. In this item, students are expected to recognize that the segment *im-* acts as a prefix.

Students can make short work of this item just by knowing that *im-* means *not*. That's because only option D uses that meaning.

Caution students not to be thrown off just because they will likely recognize other prefix meanings in the answer choices. For instance, options A and C use the words *before* and *again*, and these are meanings for the prefixes *pre-* or *re-* rather than *im-*.

✓ *Have an anchor example.*

Some students may recognize that *im-* is a prefix, but they might not be able to recall the meaning that *im-* adds as a prefix in words. These students need an example word to *anchor* their understanding.

Teach students to think of other words they know that use the prefix *im-*. If, for instance, students are able to recall the words *impatient* (for example, "I am an impatient patient when waiting for the doctor"), then they can figure out that *im-* means "not."

✓ *Construct try-out sentences, a form of substitution.*

To encourage students to consider all answer choices, have them construct try-out sentences. Because the options for this item are phrasal definitions rather than single words, students must use their judgment about how best to substitute the answer choices:

A   So I know it <u>has happened</u> that my hands have touched that ball <u>before</u>.
B   So I know it is <u>able to happen</u> that my hands will touch that ball.
C   So I know it is <u>likely to happen</u> that my hands will touch that ball <u>again</u>.
D   So I know it is <u>not likely to happen</u> that my hands will touch that ball.

Constructing try-out sentences helps students narrow the options by determining which make little sense—in this case, options A and B.

✓ *Use context clues.*

From rereading paragraph 3, in which the tested word appears, students should recognize that Jake knows Paul does not want to throw the ball to him ("But every quarterback knows not to throw the ball to the person who is consistently picked last . . ."). This detail gives meaning to the tested word—that it is "not likely to happen" that Jake will be given a chance to get his hands on that ball. Option D is correct.

Roots

> Which word from paragraph 3 contains a root word that means "to carry"?
>
> A   *transported*
> B   *consistently*
> C   *heavily*
> D   *opponent*
>
> Correct answer: A

Strategies

✓ *Locate important information in the item.*

The item tells students the following:

- What skill is being tested (key words: *root word*)
- Where the answer is located (paragraph 3)
- That the options are lifted directly from the passage (use of italics)

✓ *Know the vocabulary term.*

In this item, students must know that a root word is the fundamental part of a word to which letters can be added before and after to form new words. A root word gives the word its meaning—for example, *port*—and other word parts are what change the meaning—e.g., trans*port*ation, air*port*, *port*able.

✓ *Home in on a root.*

Students should first use their knowledge of word parts to strike out any prefixes and suffixes. Once the word parts are "decluttered," students need to apply only two principles of word construction:

1. If both a prefix and suffix are present, the root will appear in the middle.
2. If there is no prefix, the root will appear at the beginning.

Options A and B follow the first principle, so the prefix and suffix can be ignored so that students can focus on the part(s) of the word that might be a root:

A *trans* [prefix] | *port* | *ed* [suffix]
B *con* [prefix] | *sist* | *ent* [suffix] | *ly* [suffix]

(For option B, students might recognize and cross out only the *–ly* suffix, which would still be helpful.)

Options C and D follow the second principle, so the suffixes can be ignored so that students can focus on the part of the word that might be a root:

C *heav* | *ily* [suffix]
D *oppon* | *ent* [suffix]

(For option D, students might not recognize *–ent* as a suffix and cross out nothing, which would be fine.)

This simple step helps students focus on the parts of the words that may or may not be recognizable roots.

✓ *Connect the possible roots to other words and meanings.*

After using the strategy above, students should try to think of familiar words that use these same word parts as roots. For instance, in option A, students might think of the word *portable*, or they might simply recognize that the word part *port* is a word itself, as in a ship's port. For option C, students might think of the word *heavy*, and in option D, students might connect the word *oppose* to *oppon* or *opponent*.

Students can then compare their word associations to the meaning "to carry," which is what the item asks. They should recognize easily that the meanings of the words *transport*, *portable*, and *port* are variations on "to carry." Option A is the clear correct answer.

✓ *Use substitution.*

Notice how easily the word *transported* in paragraph 3 can be replaced with a variant of "to carry":

> *And then the ball pauses in mid-air while I am* carried *(in thought) back to the fourth grade.*

Because the substitution makes sense in the passage, students can feel confident that *transported* means "to carry."

Multiple-Meaning Words

Read the dictionary entry below.

catch ['kach] v. 1. to take hold of or intercept (something falling, thrown, etc.) 2. to seize or capture, especially after a pursuit 3. to attract the attention of 4. to grasp the meaning of

Which definition best matches how the word catch is used in paragraph 3?

A Definition 1
B Definition 2
C Definition 3
D Definition 4

Correct answer: C

Strategies

✓ *Recognize the item type.*

This item type approximates the experience of a student looking up a word in the dictionary and negotiating each of its meanings. Students might need to be shown a sample of this item type so that they understand what is being asked.

Some assessments present multiple-meaning words with definitions for at least two parts of speech. These items present students with a distinct advantage if they apply their knowledge of parts of speech; the answer choices that refer to parts of speech that are different from the tested word are not viable correct answers. Other assessments present only those multiple-meaning words that have four meanings with the same part of speech; for these items, knowledge of parts of speech will not help students eliminate answer choices, so students must use other strategies.

✓ *Locate important information in the item.*
The item tells students the following:

- What word is being tested (*catch*)
- Where the tested word is located (paragraph 3)

- That the dictionary entry is integral to negotiating the correct answer (key words: *read the dictionary entry below; best matches how the word* catch *is used*)

An alternate version of a multiple-meaning item is presented in Figure 3.2.

✓ *Don't be enticed by the most familiar definition.*
Most multiple-meaning items present a *familiar* word to students to see if they can recognize a meaning for that word that might be *less familiar* or *unfamiliar* to them. That is, the purpose of presenting a multiple-meaning item is not to assess if students already know the most common use of that word; the goal is to determine if students can understand that a commonly used word has different meanings in different contexts.

For the word *catch*, students are probably more familiar with the definition *to take hold of* than the definition *to attract the attention of*. Therefore, students should be mindful that they must look for the meaning that matches how the word is

FIGURE 3.2 **An Alternate Version of a Multiple-Meaning Item**

Read this sentence from paragraph 3.

Sure enough, Paul tries desperately to catch *the eye of another teammate.*

In which sentence does the word *catch* have the same meaning that it does in the sentence above?

A The children tried to catch the candy being tossed from the parade floats.
B The officer was not able to catch the criminal alone, so he called for reinforcements.
C I was searching for a painting at the art show that would catch my fancy.
D I did not catch his critical tone until later when I thought about what he had said.

used in the passage, not the definition that leaps out at them because it is familiar.

Furthermore, the definition *to take hold of* for the word *catch* fits the overall context of the passage because the setting is a baseball field—and yet this meaning is not the correct answer for this item. So, this item is a good example to show students that they must read all of the information provided in an item, refer to the passage, and allow themselves some thinking time rather than assuming that the answer must be the one that refers to the general context of baseball.

✔ Reread the targeted paragraph and use context clues to find a synonym for the tested word.

The structure of this item sets up students to read through four dictionary meanings before they read the actual question. Reading and thinking through the four dictionary meanings can be overwhelming, especially because the item does not provide the context in which the tested word is used. Therefore, students should be encouraged to return to the passage to reread the paragraph in which the tested word appears *before* they become encumbered by the four definitions.

Another good idea is for students to challenge themselves to think of a substitute for *catch* in the tested sentence. Doing so will help them begin thinking about which of the four definitions fits the context. For instance, in this item, students might choose *gain* as a synonym and substitute it: "Sure enough, Paul tries desperately to *gain* the eye of another teammate." Then students can read each of the dictionary meanings to find the one that most closely means *gain*. Option C is the best match.

✔ Construct try-out sentences with a key word from each dictionary entry.

Students can select a key word or phrase—a strong noun or verb, for instance—that sufficiently represents each dictionary entry. Then they can construct try-out sentences to determine which makes the most sense. Students might need some practice with this strategy to understand how to insert the key word or phrase into the tested sentence.

The key words from the definitions that students might consider lifting are the following:

A   *take hold of*
B   *capture*
C   *attract the attention of*
D   *grasp the meaning of*

The try-out sentences with those key words look like this:

A   Sure enough, Paul tries desperately to <u>take hold of</u> the eye of another teammate.
B   Sure enough, Paul tries desperately to <u>capture</u> the eye of another teammate.
C   Sure enough, Paul tries desperately to <u>attract the attention of</u> another teammate.
D   Sure enough, Paul tries desperately to <u>grasp the meaning of</u> another teammate.

Students can easily eliminate options A and D. Because the sentences in options B and C make some sense, students must depend on their knowledge of the context. Students have to go back to the dictionary entry to understand that *capture* in option B means literally taking control of something, which makes this meaning less viable. Students who consider that Jake is desperately trying to be noticed by the quarterback will determine that option C is the most suitable answer.

Connotation

The author uses the word <u>hustled</u> in paragraph 12 to show Jake's—

A   anxiety
B   confusion
C   enthusiasm
D   strength

Correct answer: B

Strategies

✓ *Locate important information in the item.*
The item stem tells students the following:

- What word is being tested (*hustled*)
- Where the tested word is located (paragraph 12)

✓ *Recognize the item type.*
Whereas other vocabulary item types essentially ask "*This* means *that*," items that test connotation ask students to dig deeper for the meaning of a familiar word. Connotation items ask about the impact or effect that the word has on some aspect of the passage, such as the plot or characterization.

Students should be familiar with how connotation items are worded and what students are expected to do. In this item, students must take their knowledge of the word *hustled* and apply it to Jake (narrator) and what Jake is doing (action) in order to better understand the resolution of the passage.

✓ *Use context and syntactic clues.*
From rereading paragraph 12, students should notice that the paragraph presents two important ideas, separated by the word *but* at the start of the third sentence. Essentially, the paragraph can be summed this way:

Jake is still picked last	*but*	*Jake feels differently about playing.*
(unfavorable event)	(contrasted with)	(favorable event)

Therefore, the word *hustled* has a favorable connotation, to match Jake's new outlook on playing baseball with his peers. Options A and B—which are negative emotions—must be incorrect, leaving options C and D worthy of consideration.

✓ *Try addition instead of substitution.*
Because the wording and the options of the connotation item imply that the word *hustled* tells the reader something about how Jake feels—either *anxious, confused, enthusiastic,* or *strong*—students should be able to add these words to determine if the tested sentence still makes sense:

A   . . . I put on my glove and I <u>showed anxiety and</u> hustled to right field.
B   . . . I put on my glove and I <u>showed confusion and</u> hustled to right field.
C   . . . I put on my glove and I <u>showed enthusiasm and</u> hustled to right field.
D   . . . I put on my glove and I <u>showed strength and</u> hustled to right field.

Again, options A and B are easily dismissed because they provide meanings that are opposite of how Jake feels.

Option D cannot be correct because Jake's improvement in attitude is mental, not physical; the author is not using the word *hustled* to comment on Jake's strength.

With this strategy, the sentence created using option C, *enthusiasm*, contributes most to the resolution of the passage. Jake is more encouraged and enthusiastic as a result of the prior day's events, which is represented in the connotation of the word *hustled*. Option C is correct.

Chapter 4

Important Ideas

This chapter presents information about the most common types of items that assess a basic comprehension of a text. For the purposes of grouping in this book, they are called "important ideas" and consist of the standards that pertain to main ideas, details, and summary. The following are examples, not particular to any state, of reading standards for the comprehension of important ideas. Students are expected to do the following:

- Determine a text's *main ideas*
- Recall or locate supporting *details*
- *Summarize* the major ideas of a text

Basic Strategies for Items About Important Ideas

The following basic strategies are good starting points for teachers to share with students as they work together to make sense of reading test items about important ideas. Later in this chapter, strategies that are specific to certain types of these items are explored.

✓ *Recognize the item type, locate important information in the item, and know the terms.*

Main ideas. The stem of main idea items explicitly indicates to students what is being tested, usually with the terms *main idea, mainly about,* or *mostly about.*

Stems also indicate if students are asked to identify the main idea of a single paragraph, a group of paragraphs, or the passage as a whole. A targeted paragraph(s) or sections of text will contain one clear major idea rather than competing major ideas; otherwise, there would be more than one correct answer.

Details. The words *according to the passage* are a signal to students that this item type assesses literal understandings—meaning that the answer is *literally* found in the passage. The answer in the item might be stated exactly as it appears in the passage or the idea may be paraphrased. Usually detail items contain the words *according to the passage*, but other item types can use those words as well. Students should be taught that regardless of what the item is assessing, the answer can be found in the passage when the item stem uses the words *according to the passage* or *in the passage.*

Summary. Summary items usually include the term *summary* in the item stem. These items ask about the summary of an entire passage (especially in literary passages) or a distinct section of a passage that can be summarized effectively (especially in informational passages).

✓ *Make text more manageable with the "chunk and jot down" strategy.*

Passages can be quite long on middle school assessments. When students encounter items for which they must return to the text to reread to find the answer, they can waste a lot of time and become overwhelmed merely by trying to locate where they should begin rereading. Sometimes students end up reading the entire passage again and again when they encounter several difficult items. The "chunk and jot down" strategy can help students by allowing them to section off portions of the text even before they begin trying to answer items.

Chunk. The passage "The Gym Class ~~Nobody~~ Somebody" has a structure that can be divided nicely. For instance, the first chunk that should be obvious to readers is paragraphs 1 and 2. In these paragraphs, the narrator is miserable in gym class, which is almost over. A second chunk, paragraphs 3–5, is a flashback to when the narrator fumbled the football in the fourth grade. A third chunk, paragraphs 6–11, shares the narrator's excitement and peers' praise for catching the ball. A final chunk, the last paragraph, shows that the narrator changed his attitude about gym class as a result of the experience. By drawing a line across the page to section off the text in these chunks, students can reduce a long, overwhelming passage to more reasonable, manageable chunks. Furthermore, these chunks help students focus in clearly on the author's structure.

Jot Down. As students decide on how paragraphs of text contribute to a chunk, they can identify those chunks with a short phrase or quick drawing to help them remember what happens. For paragraphs 1 and 2, for instance, a student might sum this chunk as "Narrator is miserable" and/or draw a sad face with sweat dripping down the face; the sum of the final paragraph of the passage might be "Narrator is encouraged" and/or a drawing might be of a boy in right field with his glove raised. Sometimes just a "feeling face" is enough to capture the moment. For instance, students might draw a disappointed face next to paragraph 5 to express the narrator's self-criticism, and, next to paragraph 7, an excited face would capture Jake's joy in hearing praise from peers.

With some practice, students can customize the strategy so that it's quick but effective in making a passage easier to navigate.

Main Ideas

Paragraph 2 is mostly about—

A   how a ball has been hit to Jake for the first time

B   how Jake finds his gym class to be boring

C   what Jake's teammates say to him

D   how gym class is almost over

Correct answer: A

Strategies

✓ *Recognize the item type and locate important information in the item.*

The item stem tells students the following:

- Which paragraph is targeted (paragraph 2)
- That the correct answer is the main idea of the targeted paragraph (key words: *mostly about*)

Alternate versions of main idea items are presented in Figure 4.1.

✓ *Check your notes from "chunk and jot down."*

Students who use the "chunk and jot down" strategy (described at the beginning of this chapter) during and after reading the sample passage can return to paragraph 2 to see if their notes are helpful for this item. If, for instance, students

FIGURE 4.1 **Alternate Versions of Main Idea Items**

Which of these statements is the main idea of the passage?

What is the passage mostly about?

This passage is mostly telling about—

The section titled _____ is mostly about—

Paragraphs X through X tell the reader about—

What question does the last paragraph answer?

Which paragraphs in the passage would probably have this heading: _____?

wrote "Incoming!" and/or drew a picture of a boy with his hands raised to catch a baseball, these notes might remind them that in paragraph 2, Jake realizes a ball is coming toward him. This notion matches option A.

✓ *Think big, not small.*

The correct answer to a main idea item "sounds" a certain way. A main idea is an essence, a gist, an idea that is so important that it is memorable. It is weighty. It is inextricably connected to one or more of the elements of the story—plot, character, conflict, resolution, and/or theme. It stands out. It is a big deal.

Details, on the other hand, don't hold the same weight in the story as a whole and don't connect to multiple elements of a story. For instance, when students see option D, "how gym class is almost over," they should think, "Who cares?" or "So what!" The fact is that whether there is a half hour or just a few minutes left in gym class, a baseball is headed to Jake and he had better figure out what to do. The amount of time left in gym class is a minor detail; it is not "big" enough to serve as a main idea.

By contrast, option A, "how a ball has been hit to Jake for the first time," certainly is a major event that sparks a flashback that fills in readers about how Jake feels inept on the sports field, which is also the central conflict. The option—especially with the words *for the first time*—also sounds like a big idea rather than an unimportant one, especially given students' understandings of plot.

✓ *Ask a critical question (or two).*

Students can ask themselves, "What is the one thing the author needs me to know about the information in this paragraph?" then formulate their own response and see which option it closely matches. For instance, students might say, "The author needs me to know that while Jake usually goes unnoticed in gym class, a ball has been hit in his direction and he can hardly believe it." Students might need to be reminded that the way they phrase their response will not always be similar to how the test does; nonetheless, they should be able to see the similarity between their response and option A, "how a ball has been hit to Jake for the first time."

A version of that critical question is, for this item, "What would I *not* know if paragraph 2 wasn't there?" Students could read paragraph 1 and then jump to read paragraph 3. By doing so, they would realize that Jake is invisible in gym class in paragraph 1, but in paragraph 3, Jake has a memory of another time when he had a chance to catch a ball. So the main idea of paragraph 2 must be the notion that something happens to cause Jake to have the memory that begins in paragraph 3—which is that he is faced with having to catch a ball. Option A captures that notion.

✓ *Build a case.*

Students should be able to point to phrases and sentences within the targeted paragraph that support the correct answer, while also finding a dearth of evidence to support the other options, as shown in Figure 4.2.

Option A captures the fact that an unexpected event is taking place (". . . something happens that has never happened before") and that a ball has been hit to Jake ("There is a fly ball heading my way . . ." and "A baseball is indeed heading toward me . . .").

Option B has no solid evidence from the targeted paragraph. It actually captures the main idea of paragraph 1, not paragraph 2, so students should be certain to direct their attention to the targeted paragraph in main idea items.

Option C has little evidence except for the actual quotes, which compose only two sentences in the paragraph. Furthermore, paragraph 2 is

FIGURE 4.2 **Options and Supporting Evidence**

Options	Supporting Evidence
A a ball has been hit to Jake for the first time	". . . something happens that has never happened before." "There is a fly ball heading my way . . ." "A baseball is indeed heading toward me . . ."
B gym class is boring	Evidence is from previous paragraph: "Every day is the same . . ."
C Jake's teammates say something to him	"'Get under it, Jake,' someone commands." "'Don't be scared of it,' someone else hollers."
D gym class is almost over	" . . . with 3 minutes and 42 seconds remaining . . ."

clearly about Jake and his thinking, so option C, which is about the teammates rather than about Jake, cannot suffice as a main idea.

Option D should be the least tempting option. It is an attractive choice only to students who believe in what might be called the "main idea item myth"—that the correct answer can be found in the first sentence of the targeted paragraph. Although Jake might be happy that gym class is almost over (given the information provided in the previous paragraph), how much time remains in gym class fails to tell readers about the actual events taking place. Option D is a minor—not major—idea.

The "build a case" strategy highlights that when only one sentence or only a portion of a sentence can be found (or stretched!) to support an option, it is likely that the option is a minor detail rather than an important idea. Multiple sentences or multiple parts of sentences can usually be found to support a main idea, which in this case is option A.

Details

> According to the passage, what is Jake fiddling with while on the baseball field?
>
> A   His glove
> B   His watch
> C   A football
> D   A whistle
>
> Correct answer: B

Strategies

✓ *Recognize the item type.*

The words *according to the passage* signal that this item assesses literal understandings—meaning, the answer is addressed specifically in the passage rather than requiring inferential thinking.

✓ *Hunt and point.*

To answer detail items, students should be encouraged to return to the passage to hunt down the answer, even if they think they recall the answer. Using the "chunk and jot down" strategy described in the introduction to this chapter, students can use information in the item stem to know that they need to return to the part of the story that is set on a baseball field. Students should be able to recall that there are four settings: the baseball field, the football field, the locker room, and math class. By chunking the passage by setting, students should be able to determine that the answer appears either in paragraphs 1 to 2 or 6 to 7 or in paragraph 12.

Students should also be able to recall that Jake is likely "fiddling with" something early in the story, when he is bored because he is invisible on the baseball field. The information needed to answer this item is stated in paragraph 1: "I wind the dial of my watch and tap on it, thinking the second hand has stopped moving." Winding it, tapping on it, and staring at it are clues that Jake fiddles with his watch while he is bored on the baseball field, making option B the correct answer.

✓ *Hunt in vain for the wrong options.*

For detail items—and items that use the phrase *according to the passage*—it makes sense that students can hunt for and point to the correct answer in the passage. Because there can be only one correct answer, students should also be able to read the three wrong options and *not* find anything they can point to in the passage to support those options.

As a way of confirming their choice for the correct answer, students should try to hunt for and point to any information in the passage that could support options A, C, or D. By working through each option, students should realize that they cannot find these ideas literally stated in the passage. That is, there is no information that supports that Jake is fiddling with his glove; in fact, paragraph 1 says that he takes it off because he thinks he will not need it. Options C and D are objects that appear in other parts of the story—a football is part of the fourth-grade flashback, and the whistle belongs to the coach, not Jake—so these options do not have anything to do with the baseball field. Therefore, because all three options can be eliminated, option B is confirmed as the clear correct answer.

Summary

Which of these is the best summary of the passage?

A   While it is usually unexciting, gym class changes everything for Jake one day.

B   The heat and blinding sun usually make gym class miserable for Jake, but he promises not to let the conditions bother him when playing baseball.

C   For Jake, gym class is simply something that must be endured.

D   Gym class is wearisome for Jake and even brings back a bad memory, except when he achieves star status, even if only for one day.

Correct answer: D

Strategies

✓ *Recognize the item type.*

The word *summary* tells students that their ability to summarize is being assessed. A summary expresses the main ideas and most important supporting details without including minor details. Answer choices might be structured as one sentence or multiple sentences.

✓ *Check your notes from "chunk and jot down."*

The "chunk and jot down" strategy (described at the beginning of this chapter) is ideal for helping students with summary items. By reflecting on how the passage can be divided into sensible chunks and reviewing their summary notes and illustrations, students are reminded of the overall direction of the passage and can use the information as a starting point for determining the best summary.

✓ *Look for completeness.*

The correct answer for a summary item is the one that most completely tells about the passage or section of text. In informational passages, options that fail to cover several important aspects of a topic are incorrect. In literary passages, options that fail to make reference to the major literary elements of plot, setting, problem, resolution, and theme are incorrect.

Literary nonfiction passages can be tricky, because summarizing the essence of the passage requires special attention to the narrator's feelings or attitude changes in addition to the major literary elements. Still, the wrong options will tell only part of the story. For instance, option C, "For Jake, gym class is simply something that must be endured," tells about Jake's initial feelings ("I stand, unnoticed"; "I wait for gym class to be over" [paragraph 1]), but does not show a change in Jake's attitude that occurs in the last paragraph as a result of catching the ball. In this respect, option C is vastly insufficient as a summary.

Options might be infused with minor details rather than major plot events, which make them incorrect. In option B, for instance, the words "The heat and blinding sun usually make gym class miserable for Jake" represent details from paragraphs 1 and 2. But these details are not as important as how Jake feels on the baseball field, which is "unnoticed" (paragraph 1) and "lost" (paragraph 2). Students should be careful not to be tempted by minor details in summary options.

Inaccurate information or an overstated idea can also make an option incorrect. An option might be a combination of a couple of true plot events and one or more misinterpretations of other events for narrative passages, or a combination of one major point and a misread of another main point in informational passages. In option A, ". . . gym class changes everything for Jake one day," the words *changes everything* are an overstatement of what happens and how Jake feels. While Jake's attitude about participating in gym class has changed, "everything" has not, especially considering that Jake is still picked last and still plays right field. Because an important idea is overstated, option A cannot be correct.

✓ Put key pieces together.

Try story elements. With a typical narrative structure, students can think about the key pieces of the story to help them focus on the main literary elements:

Setting + Main Character + Problem + Solution Attempts + Solution = Summary

Because this passage is a personal essay, students might have to think of the major parts in other ways.

Try settings. One way students might conceptualize the most important parts of the text is to think about the changes in settings:

Baseball Field (day one) + Football Field + Math Class + Baseball Field (day two).

Using this strategy, students might be led to option D as the correct answer:

Gym class is wearisome for Jake [baseball field—day one] and even brings back a bad memory [football field], except when he achieves star status [math class], even if only for one day [baseball field—day two].

Try characterization and dramatic structure. For first-person autobiographical reflections, the most important parts pertain to an author's feelings and changes. These feelings and changes are usually explored over the course of the passage, so students can think about dividing the major events into three of the main parts of a dramatic structure—rising action, climax, and falling action. Using this strategy, students might be led to option D:

Gym class is wearisome for Jake [bad feelings—rising action] and even brings back a bad memory [bad feelings—rising action], except when he achieves star status [change in

feelings to pride—climax], even if only for one day [falling action].

Furthermore, students should realize that an essential part of this passage is the flashback that informs readers about Jake's past feelings about playing sports with his peers. That flashback is so important that a complete summary would need to address what the reader learns about Jake as a result of the memory. Only option D addresses the flashback, which is another indication that this option is the most complete one.

✓ Analyze each option for key words that relate to important literary elements.

Students can analyze each option to detect key words that signify literary elements as well as details or events that are posing as more important than they are. Look how each option can be labeled:

A While it is usually unexciting [problem], gym class changes everything for Jake one day [misrepresented outcome].

B The heat and blinding sun [minor detail] usually make gym class miserable for Jake [misrepresented problem], but he promises not to let the conditions bother him [misrepresented outcome] when playing baseball.

C For Jake, gym class is simply something that must be endured [problem].

D Gym class is wearisome for Jake [problem] and even brings back a bad memory [explains and adds to problem], except when he achieves star status [important plot event and change], even if only for one day [outcome].

By attempting to label each part of an option, students can recognize that only option D avoids minor details in favor of including other major plot events and important literary elements, such as character change and story resolution, and is therefore complete and correct.

Chapter 5

Literary Elements

This chapter presents information about the most common types of items used to assess literary elements on state assessments. These include plot, character (including traits, motivations, relationships, conflicts, and changes), setting, problem/tension/conflict, solution/resolution, and theme/moral. The following are examples, not particular to any state, of reading standards for literary elements. Students are expected to do the following:

- Recognize and analyze story *plot*
- Determine *characters' traits, motivations, and changes* by what the characters say and do and by how the author presents them
- Identify the *setting* and its importance to a text
- Recognize and analyze the story *problem* and *resolution*
- Determine the story *theme(s)*

Basic Strategies for Literary Elements Items

The following basic strategies are good starting points for teachers to share with students as they work together to make sense of reading test items about literary elements. Later in this chapter, strategies that are specific to certain types of these literary elements items are explored.

✓ *Recognize the item type and know the literary elements.*

Plot. Plot items do not usually use the word *plot* or any other particular word in the stem to indicate to students that their knowledge of the plot is being assessed. However, plot items typically present one specific event in the stem, and the task is for students to connect it to another important plot event. Because plot items usually cover important aspects of the plot rather than minor events that are easily skipped over by a reader, the event posed in the stem should be relatively easy for students to locate in the passage. Usually the key to answering a plot item correctly is locating the event in the passage in order to make the necessary connection between the event in the item stem and the event in the correct answer.

Character. Items testing characterization come in many forms. On most assessments, characterization can include traits (how a character feels or behaves), motivations (why a character behaves in a certain way), relationships (how a character reacts and responds to other characters), problems/conflicts (the challenges a character faces), and changes (how a character is changed or acts differently as a result of some event).

Character items usually include a key word in the item stem, such as *feels* or *changes*, to indicate to students which aspect of characterization is being assessed. The options of character items usually contain "feeling words," so students can identify the item type this way as well.

Character items do not usually ask about minor or flat characters. When minor characters are included in items, they are usually there to assess how those minor characters affect the main characters (i.e., character relationships). Students should recognize that minor characters usually help to move the plot along by engaging main characters in some action or dialogue.

Setting. The stems of setting items usually include the words *setting* or *takes place* to indicate to students that their ability to recognize setting is being assessed. On middle school assessments, setting items usually require students to go beyond simply identifying the setting. Such items ask about the importance of the setting to the story; in other words, students are required to consider how setting contributes to another important literary element, such as plot or problem. For instance, some problems in a story occur because characters find themselves in a certain setting; without that setting, there would not be a problem. Certainly these items are challenging because they require analysis.

Conflict. Items assessing conflict may include the word *problem* or *conflict* in the item stem. On middle school assessments, students will be expected to identify and/or analyze both internal and external conflicts.

Resolution. Some state assessments use the words *solve*, *solution*, and *resolution* to assess students' knowledge of resolution, so students should be familiar with these terms. Students should also be taught to think about how a text's structure might give clues about the location of the answer. For instance, in a narrative with a problem-solution text structure, the resolution is likely presented toward the end of the passage. Some assessments also ask about the turning point; students should recognize that the turning point is the event that moves the conflict toward resolution.

Theme. Items assessing theme may use the word *theme* or may ask about a text's *lesson* (especially if the intent is for the reader to learn from a lesson a main character or narrator learns), *message* (especially if the passage is classic/traditional literature, such as a folktale), or *moral* (especially if the passage is a fable). Students should know that any of these terms can be used in an item that assesses their knowledge of theme.

✓ *Use the "chunk and jot down" strategy and text structure and genre.*

Whether an event, feeling, or problem from the passage is used in the stem or the options, tracking it down in the passage is always a good idea. These elements exist within a certain context, and it is important to have clarity about that context. Using the "chunk and jot down" strategy, which is discussed near the beginning of Chapter 4, students can access the parts of the passage that likely indicate or imply the answer to items about literary elements. For instance, if a plot item asks about Jake's experience with Paul on the football field, students can review chunks of text that mention Paul.

Students' knowledge of text structure and genre also help them answer items about literary elements. For instance, students who have knowledge of a problem-solution structure of narratives can use what they know to access items about character, conflict, and resolution. Students who have read, enjoyed, and discussed memoir will know that authors typically take on important moments in their lives and reflect on and explain what happened and how these experiences affected them.

✓ *Look for connection and truth.*

Events or ideas that are used as options in literary elements items can be incorrect for a number of reasons. For instance, a true event from the story that is presented as an option can be wrong because it doesn't relate to the idea posed in the stem (e.g., *Jake talks to the coach after gym class* [true event] *because—he does not enjoy playing right field* [true event but does not relate to the idea in the stem]). Or an event used as an option can be misrepresented (a little or a lot) and is therefore incorrect (e.g., *In fourth grade, Jake is embarrassed after—being selected last for a team* [Jake is usually selected last, but he is embarrassed because he fumbles the ball]). These posers can be detected by returning to the passage to try to locate them. In the process of not finding them, students will likely uncover that the options are unrelated or misrepresented ideas, which invalidates them.

✓ *Think for yourself before letting the items cloud your thinking.*

Students who are able to make some sense of the passage before they encounter the items are often afforded a running start, especially for literary elements items. For instance, in a literary passage, students should expect to be asked questions about the main literary elements—plot, character, setting, problem, solution, and theme—and they are wise to think about the structure that the author uses for presenting these elements. So, students who answer "How?" "What?" and "Why?" are likely to home in on the most important aspects of a literary text. A student might sum the passage this way:

> *Through a flashback to an embarrassing playground experience in fourth grade, the author helps readers understand why Jake loathes middle school gym class until the day when he catches a ball and is praised by his peers. Readers learn from his experience that it's best to have a positive attitude toward things that you might not naturally enjoy.*

With this basic understanding, students are well on their way to answering correctly many of the sample items in this chapter and others as well. So, savvy test takers take a few moments to reflect on their thinking about a passage before encountering the many ideas presented in the items.

Plot

On the playground in the fourth grade, Jake is thrown the football because—

A   the teacher demands that all students get to play

B   he does not have far to run to make a touchdown

C   the quarterback cannot find anyone else who is open

D   the quarterback feels bad for picking him last

Correct answer: C

Strategies

✓ *Recognize the item type.*

Although the word *plot* does not usually appear in the stem, a plot item does usually refer to a specific event (for example, *In the fourth grade, Jake is thrown the football*). Students can use this information to determine the section of the passage that will likely lead to the answer.

You might notice that this sample plot item has a structure that is similar to cause-effect items. That is because plot items on the middle school level may ask students to identify the relationship of one event to another. Cause-effect items usually require more analysis.

✓ *Find the event in the passage.*

Because the answer to a plot item must be a true event in the passage, students should be able to return to the passage to track down the answer.

Students should recognize that paragraphs 3 through 5 describe Jake's memory of fourth grade. The answer must lie in these paragraphs because the event in this item's stem appears in these paragraphs. By rereading the end of paragraph 4 and the beginning of paragraph 5, students should determine that the quarterback throws the ball to Jake because Jake is the only one who is not heavily guarded. Option C is the answer.

✓ *Look for connection and truth.*

Plot items essentially ask students to determine which of four statements completes or relates to the plot event mentioned in the stem. For plot items to have rigor, the wrong options are usually details or events from the passage that have been twisted around a bit so that they do not correspond to the event posed in the stem. In other words, instead of offering, "During recess in the fourth grade, Jake is thrown the football because *he is wearing a bright shirt*," which is a ridiculous choice, the item poses that the teacher demands that all students get to play (option A). This option takes a statement—that everyone is allowed to play during recess because the teacher is watching—and twists it around so that it is inaccurate—the quarterback is not prompted to throw the ball to Jake because of a teacher. Readers who are not paying close attention might choose this option because they remember reading something about how a teacher makes sure that everyone gets to play. Careful test takers can write "does not happen" next to options if they can justify that an event has been presented inaccurately, as shown in Figure 5.1.

The idea in option C is the only one that pertains to Jake's experience on the playground in the fourth grade.

FIGURE 5.1 **Options and Justification**

Options	Justification
A the teacher demands that all students get to play	A *Does not happen.* (The teacher is not yet mentioned.)
B he does not have far to run to make a touchdown	B *Does not happen.* (While Jake might not have far to run, this is not the reason the quarterback throws the ball to Jake.)
C the quarterback cannot find anyone else who is open	C *Does happen.*
D the quarterback feels bad for picking him last	D *Does not happen.* (No information suggests that Paul gives Jake a chance because he feels bad.)

Character

In the passage, Jake changes from feeling—

A   cowardly to brave
B   unpopular to popular
C   disinterested to interested in baseball
D   hostile to friendly with his peers

Correct answer: C

Strategies

✓ *Recognize the item type.*

Two words in the stem, *changes* and *feeling*, identify this item as assessing characterization, specifically, character change.

This item looks more complicated than other types of character items. That is, many character items simply ask students to select one trait among four that describes a character. In this item, there are double that—eight trait words! It doesn't seem logical, but this item type can sometimes be easier for students than character items that offer fewer words. If students can determine that one of the two trait words does not adequately describe Jake, then the option can be eliminated. Students don't have that advantage with items that have only one word choice.

Alternate versions of character items are presented in Figure 5.2.

FIGURE 5.2 **Alternate Versions of Character Items**

Why does Jake change his attitude about _____?

How does Jake change at the end of the passage?

Unlike (another character), Jake is—

When Jake goes to gym class the next day, he most likely feels—

Jake's relationship with his coach is best described as—

✓ *Use knowledge of text features and major plot events to question the options.*

While this item tests characterization, students can benefit from their knowledge of other text features in order to help them. For instance, students will likely recognize that this piece is written in first person and that the text type is memoir or personal experience essay. Their experience with these types of texts might help them remember that usually a change of some kind, usually in attitude or perspective, takes place. Students could even conceptualize the text structure as problem-solution, albeit loosely defined. That is, Jake's problem is that he is ignored during gym class, and that changes (the solution, in loose terms) when he catches a ball and is praised by his peers, causing him to want to do better the next day. Therefore, students' knowledge of several text features can get them to think in the right direction, so to speak, for this item.

But there's another possibility for students who cannot drum up these text features. Students can think simply in terms of beginning, middle, and end in order to think about a change in a character's or narrator's feelings. Often change in a character develops through the passage, so a character might feel one way at the beginning and then another way in the middle or toward the end of the passage. This is certainly the case in this passage.

Students can use the basic question "When does Jake feel _____?" to help guide their thinking about the feeling words in the options. Then they can return to the passage to track down a major plot event to support the answers, as shown in Figure 5.3.

According to the answers to the guiding questions, option C presents two feelings that describe Jake. Those feelings also present a change—from feeling disinterested to feeling interested—and

FIGURE 5.3 Questioning the Options and Supporting the Options

Questioning the Options	Supporting the Options
A When does Jake feel *cowardly?*	*Never.*
When does Jake feel *brave?*	*Maybe when he catches the ball?*
B When does Jake feel *unpopular?*	*Maybe at the beginning?*
When does Jake feel *popular?*	*Maybe in math class, but not in the last paragraph.*
C When does Jake feel *disinterested?*	*At the beginning; he wants gym class to be over.*
When does Jake feel *interested?*	*At the end; he wants to try harder.*
D When does Jake feel *hostile?*	*This word doesn't really describe Jake.*
When does Jake feel *friendly?*	*This word doesn't really describe Jake.*

they occur at different parts of the passage—at the beginning and at the end. And those feelings fit with the text features—feeling disinterested at first and then having an experience that causes a change in attitude toward feeling interested about baseball. Option B seems correct on many levels.

When students have to use words like *maybe* and *never* as the answers to their guiding questions, as shown in Figure 5.3, they are considering the answer choices with the depth that is needed to determine the correct answer. The feeling words that are used to describe a possible change in Jake are inadequate. For instance, in option A, the words *cowardly* and *brave* seem too strong to describe Jake's feelings. The same goes for option D, in which the words *hostile* and *friendly* miss the mark. Students would have a difficult time finding supporting sentences in the passage to justify these answer choices.

Therefore, option B is revealed as the clear correct answer as a result of asking and answering questions about the two feelings (a strategy that can be used for character items with one-word options as well).

Setting

The outdoor settings in the passage help to establish—

A   why sports do not appeal to Jake
B   why Jake prefers to be left alone
C   how Jake feels when he is at school
D   how Jake admires his athletic classmates

Correct answer: A

Strategies

✓ *Recognize the item type and know common literary elements well.*

The word *settings* in the item stem indicates that this item tests knowledge of story setting. On middle school assessments, students may be asked how setting influences another literary element, such as plot or conflict.

The words *help to establish* in the item stem hint that students must analyze the impact of the settings rather than merely identify them.

✓ *Identify first, then analyze.*

Students must use the words *the outdoor settings* to recognize that the item is referring to the baseball field and the football field, or the fourth-grade playground. Once students have identified these settings, they must link these settings to the important plot events that occur in these places in order to understand how the author uses them.

✓ *Ask a key question.*

Items that ask students to analyze the setting(s) require them to think about setting in connection with at least one other story element. In the case of this item, thinking about how the setting affects the plot works well, and in other cases, how the setting contributes to the problem might work well. Formulating a key question to link one or more story elements in order to illuminate the impact of the setting(s) can help students focus on the correct answer, as shown in Figure 5.4. In this item, option A best captures the notion that the settings help readers understand why Jake finds sports unappealing.

FIGURE 5.4 **Key Questions About Setting**

Does what happens (plot) on the baseball and football fields (setting) tell readers . . .	
A why sports do not appeal to Jake	*Yes. Jake's experiences in sports explain why he feels inadequate.*
B why Jake prefers to be left alone	*No. Jake doesn't want to be left alone! He wants to be noticed.*
C how Jake feels when he is at school	*Yes and no. Jake's experiences tell how he feels about sports, but they do not provide a full picture of how he feels when he is at school.*
D how Jake admires his athletic classmates	*No. The reader learns very little about what Jake thinks about his teammates.*

Conflict

What is the conflict presented in paragraphs 3 and 4?

A   Paul cannot understand what Jake is saying.

B   Jake struggles to convince Paul to give him a chance.

C   The teacher forces Paul to pick Jake for his team.

D   Jake does not think that Paul is a good quarterback.

Correct answer: B

Strategies

✔ *Recognize the item type.*

Students are expected to recognize the key word *conflict* in order to recognize what is being assessed in this item. Students may be asked about an internal or external conflict, and/or they might have to identify the source of conflict, such as individual versus self (or authority, nature, society, technology, and so on).

✔ *Weed out problems that aren't problems.*

For a conflict item to have rigor, students will encounter four options that appear to be realistic problems. For instance, option A, "Paul cannot understand what Jake is saying," might sound like a real problem at first. Yet, while Jake does yell, "I'm open" to Paul, the author never indicates that Paul has trouble understanding what is being said; in fact, Paul is presented as intentionally ignoring Jake.

Sometimes minor details or minor plot events sound like more of a problem than they really are. For instance, option C, "The teacher forces Paul to pick Jake for his team," might stick out to students as a real-life experience that nonathletic kids face on the playground. But the information about the teacher—a part of only one sentence—is a minor detail, and the reader is not told that Paul is forced to pick Jake.

✔ *Think about the event that causes tension.*

The conflict in a story is created by causing tension. Story problems drive plot. Students should use this knowledge to think about which option accurately poses a problem for the main character or narrator.

Option A, "Paul cannot understand what Jake is saying," is not the source of tension in paragraphs 3 and 4 because the narrator conveys that Paul is choosing to disregard him.

Option B, "Jake struggles to convince Paul to give him a chance," is a reasonable source of tension and explains why Jake is going to such lengths to capture Paul's attention. In paragraphs 3 and 4, Jake wants to be given a chance to succeed, but he is doubtful that Paul will oblige.

Option C, "The teacher forces Paul to pick Jake for his team," is not a tense moment; despite a passing reference, paragraphs 3 and 4 are not about how the teacher makes a quarterback pick his team.

Option D, "Jake does not think that Paul is a good quarterback," is not the source of tension, because paragraphs 3 and 4 do not contain Jake's assessment of Paul as a quarterback.

Turning Point

The turning point of the passage occurs when—

A Jake catches the baseball
B Jake fumbles the football
C Jake talks to his coach
D Jake's teammates tell him what to do

Correct answer: A

Strategies

✓ *Recognize the item type.*

The term *turning point* indicates the skill being assessed. Students should know all the terms and definitions that relate to dramatic structure, including *climax, resolution, solution,* and *outcome.*

✓ *Look for change.*

Students might think of the turning point as the point at which everything starts to get either better or worse. In order to determine the turning point, students must first articulate the conflict—Jake is discounted by his peers on the sports field. Because the conflict builds to the climax or turning point, students can question each option to determine if a particular event causes the conflict to *turn and point* toward a resolution:

A Does Jake's conflict start to resolve because he catches the ball? (*Yes!*)
B Does Jake's conflict start to resolve because Jake fumbles the ball? (*No.*)
C Does Jake's conflict start to resolve because he talks to the coach? (*No.*)
D Does Jake's conflict start to resolve because his teammates tell him what to do? (*No.*)

Simply put, Jake changes from being unnoticed (conflict) to being noticed by his peers when he catches the baseball (turning point). Option A is the correct answer.

✓ *Think about dramatic structure.*

Another approach for determining the turning point is to think about dramatic structure. By plotting the conflict and resolution, students can determine which event makes sense as a shift from the conflict toward the resolution, as shown in Figure 5.5. Option A fits nicely as the turning point in this diagram of the plot structure. When combined with the rising and falling action, a complete picture of the passage is provided.

FIGURE 5.5 **Dramatic Structure**

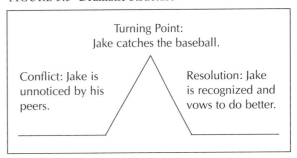

Theme

Which statement expresses the theme of the passage?

A   Appreciate the time you spend with your friends.

B   In difficult situations, take a positive approach.

C   Avoid taking on more responsibility than you can handle.

D   In competitive sports, the most important thing is winning.

Correct answer: B

Strategies

✓ *Recognize the item type.*

The word *theme* indicates that students must uncover an important theme in the passage.

Alternate versions of theme items are presented in Figure 5.6.

✓ *Be familiar with themes.*

Often students need explicit instruction about what a theme of a story is and how the author helps readers arrive at that theme. A theme is the "take-away knowledge"—it is what the author wants the reader to take away from the reading experience, to turn over in the mind, to apply to one's own life experiences. Themes often "sound"

a certain way—sometimes like good advice from one person to another.

In theme items, students must decipher which theme fits the story from among several other themes. Students have to guard against being lulled into thinking that an answer choice is "close enough." All options will likely tempt students in some way (so as not to be far-fetched and easily dismissed), but only one option will be closely connected to the passage and therefore correct.

Figure 5.7 provides a short list of categories of themes as well as possibilities for how those themes might be worded on a reading assessment.

FIGURE 5.6 **Alternate Versions of Theme Items**

What lesson does [narrator or main character] learn?

What message does the author want readers to know?

What is most likely the author's message?

In this story, the [narrator or main character] learns a lesson about—

What is the moral of this story? (specifically for fables)

FIGURE 5.7 **Common Themes and Examples**

Overcoming challenges	Facing challenges can teach you about yourself. Challenges can often be overcome with hard work and patience.
Facing fears and failure	Facing the unknown can teach us a great deal about ourselves. Everyone makes mistakes, so choose to learn from them.
Being an individual	Stand up for what you believe in. Find what your talent is and share it with others.
Change	Change is often difficult at first. Adjusting to something new takes time.
Being charitable	Giving to others is often the best reward. Share with others what you have.
Acceptance	Accept, don't judge, those around you. Accept what you have and make the most of it.
Friendships	Value your friendships. Friends can help you get through hard times.
Family	Families love you no matter what. Families teach us about ourselves and our lives.

✔ *Focus on key words and ask key questions.*

By focusing on key words in the options, students can begin to determine which theme is the most applicable to the passage as a whole:

A Appreciate the time you spend with your friends.

B In difficult situations, take a positive approach.

C Avoid taking on more responsibility than you can handle.

D In competitive sports, the most important thing is winning.

Furthermore, because a theme of a literary passage usually relates to a main character, students can formulate key questions about how the narrator (or main character) relates to the key words:

A Does Jake appreciate the time he spends with friends?

B Does Jake face difficult situations? Does Jake take a positive approach?

C Does Jake learn to avoid taking on more responsibility than he can handle?

D Does Jake learn from sports that winning is the most important thing?

By underlining key words and asking key questions, students should recognize that option B cap-

tures both the narrator's main problem (he finds it difficult to endure sports) and the outcome (he decides to take a more positive approach to baseball). "In difficult situations, take a positive approach" is a "big idea," or the "take-away knowledge," that readers can learn from Jake's experience.

✔ *Build a case.*

To build a case for a theme is to collect events from the passage that specifically relate to that theme. This strategy helps students take a discerning eye to each option; usually, students discover that there is far less evidence to support an answer choice than they might think.

For instance, option A, "Appreciate the time you spend with your friends," might appeal to students at first, especially because they likely agree with the statement and/or because the last paragraph suggests that Jake will try to be more collegial with his peers on the sports field. But if students build a case by looking for three pieces of evidence to support that theme, they will likely come up empty-handed.

The same goes for the other options, as illustrated in Figure 5.8.

Option B presents a theme that can be supported by evidence from the passage.

FIGURE 5.8 **Support and Justification for a Theme**

Option	Support and Justification
A Appreciate the time you spend with your friends.	*Not supported. While Jake likely enjoys the attention in math class, his experience doesn't illustrate the importance of friendship.*
B In difficult situations, take a positive approach.	*Supported. Jake's experience teaches him to have a positive attitude even in areas that aren't easy. The last paragraph shows that he has adopted a more positive outlook.*
C Avoid taking on more responsibility than you can handle.	*Not supported. Jake's experience isn't about personal responsibility; this idea is unrelated to Jake's experience.*
D In competitive sports, the most important thing is winning.	*Not supported. While Jake wants to try harder, his experience doesn't illustrate that winning is everything.*

Chapter 6

Literary Techniques

This chapter presents information about the most common types of items used to assess literary techniques on state assessments. Because literary techniques are typically grouped within one standard, the following is an example of a literary techniques standard, not particular to any state. Students are expected to do the following:

- Recognize and apply meaning to literary techniques such as figurative language use, simile, metaphor, personification, hyperbole, analogy, flashback, foreshadowing, symbolism, mood/tone, and style in a variety of reading passages.

Basic Strategies for Literary Techniques Items

The following basic strategies are good starting points for teachers to share with students as they work together to make sense of reading test items about literary techniques. Later in this chapter, strategies that are specific to certain types of literary techniques items are explored.

✓ *Recognize the item type and locate important information in the item.*

The words, phrases, or sentences that compose literary techniques are not usually emphasized in a special way in the passages (such as through using underlining or quotation marks). Therefore, students should use the paragraph references provided in the item stem to return to the passage to find the example of the literary technique being tested. To stay focused on the example, students might choose to underline or circle it.

Some assessments approach literary techniques items in quite generic ways, such as by using the words *The author uses this phrase to mean. . . .* Other times, item stems specifically mention the literary technique being tested, as in *The author uses a metaphor in paragraph 1 to show. . . .* Students should be shown examples of item stems that are written in ways that both generically and specifically indicate that literary techniques are being assessed.

✓ *Know the literary techniques well.*

There are essentially two types of literary techniques items: those that ask students to identify the technique and those that ask students to interpret the meaning of the use.

It seems logical that identification items are easier than interpretive items, but the opposite can be true. If students cannot identify the literary technique as such, they have little hope of getting the item correct. On the other hand, students can often bring multiple strategies to interpretive items and have a better chance of accessing the meaning of an example of a particular technique.

Therefore, in all cases, students who know well the literary techniques mentioned in the curriculum's reading standards are usually able to access both types of items. For most items, what constitutes knowing a technique well means being able to define the technique and bring meaning to an example of it. Students need many opportunities to identify and interpret literary techniques in various contexts during classroom reading and instruction.

✓ *Have anchor examples.*

In addition to being able to call up simple definitions of literary techniques, students can use examples to help them identify or interpret the literary techniques in items. Students should be taught how to extrapolate what they need from the anchor example they choose to learn well. For instance, students who choose "Her voice is as annoying as fingernails on a chalkboard" as their anchor example of simile should recognize from the example that a simile is a comparison between two things that uses the word *as* (or *like*). By being able to refer to an anchor example, students have a better chance of accessing the information they need to answer an item about that literary technique. The activities in Section 4 allow students to explore and settle on their anchor examples of various literary techniques.

✓ *Use context.*

Students will *not* have all the information they need in the item stem and answer choices for literary techniques items that require interpretations; that is why a paragraph or section reference appears in these types of items. An item stem, for the sake of brevity, isolates the example of a literary technique, so it is important for students to return to the passage and reread enough of the surrounding text to understand the context. Often the context in which the literary technique "lives" is the best key to interpreting its meaning.

Figurative Language

Read this sentence from paragraph 12.

Now, this is the part of the story where I wish I could tell you that my status took roots.

The figurative phrase "I wish I could tell you that my status took roots" means the narrator wishes—

A   he developed an interest in gardening
B   he became popular with girls
C   his knowledge of baseball increased
D   his glory as an athlete continued to grow

Correct answer: D

Strategies

✔ Locate important information in the item.

The item tells students the following:

- What sentence is being tested (. . . *I wish I could tell you that my status took roots*)
- Where the sentence is located in the passage (paragraph 12)

✔ Recognize the item type.

The term *figurative phrase* indicates that this item asks students to interpret figurative language. However, not all figurative language items are clearly marked in this way; some items may provide a sentence and ask for the meaning, leaving students to recognize that they are being asked to ascribe a literal meaning to a figurative phrase. As a result, students need multiple exposures to figurative language items.

In this item, students must recognize that the lifted text (. . . *I wish I could tell you that my status took roots*) creates an image that is not meant literally—nothing is literally growing roots into the ground. Students then must figure out from the context what the interesting use of language means.

✔ Get a general feel for the use of figurative language.

Figurative language has either a favorable or an unfavorable connotation connected to it. For instance, the idioms "in hot water" and "stabbed in the back" convey unfavorable meanings—and students can often figure this out without needing context clues.

Students should be encouraged, as a starting point, to decide if the use of figurative language being tested is intended to be favorable or unfavorable in meaning. In this item, students will likely determine that something that is rooted is usually strong and solid, so the phrase likely has a positive meaning. Any options that express negative ideas could easily be eliminated. While items assessing the interpretation of figurative language sometimes offer a mix of positive and negative interpretations, that is not the case with this item, so students have to use other strategies.

✔ Use context clues to reword the sentence.

Even if students have no conception of the figurative meaning in the tested sentence, they can use information in paragraph 12 to figure out the answer. Students can reread the paragraph, thinking about the intended meaning, and then try to reword the sentence to convert it from a figurative meaning to a literal meaning.

By rereading paragraph 12, students should first home in on what the author means by the word *status*: Readers likely understand that because Jake's peers talk about his catch that day in math class, Jake is enjoying the spotlight. By saying that he wished his status "took roots," it makes sense that Jake would want that status to grow even stronger and greater. The next sentence, which begins with a clear clue, "The truth is," indicates that his celebrity status did not endure because he returns to being chosen last. All of these context clues should help students understand the meaning of the figurative use of the words *took roots*. Students should use this information to reword the sentence, replacing the figurative use with a literal meaning. One version of the sentence might be *Now, this is the part of the story where I wish I could tell you that my status <u>became stronger and greater</u>*. Then they can match their response with the one option that is closest in meaning, which is "continued to grow" in option D.

✓ *Use substitution.*

Students can use substitution to help them confirm their hunch about the correct answer. Each answer choice can be substituted for the figurative phrase:

A . . . I wish I could tell you that I *developed an interest in gardening*. The truth is that the next day, I . . . was chosen—last.

B . . . I wish I could tell you that I *became popular with girls*. The truth is that the next day, I . . . was chosen—last.

C . . . I wish I could tell you that *my knowledge of baseball increased*. The truth is that the next day, I . . . was chosen—last.

D . . . I wish I could tell you that *my glory as an athlete continued to grow*. The truth is that the next day, I . . . was chosen—last.

This strategy, combined with reading enough of the context to give the sentence meaning, helps students to see that options A, B, and C make little sense. Option A is an awkward attempt at a literal meaning of the words *took roots*, so it should be the least tempting. Options B and C are at least related to the events in the passage, but they become less viable when the sentence that follows ("The truth is . . .") is taken into account. Option D best expresses that notion that Jake just wants to remain noticed by his peers, but returns to being picked last again; he has not been able to maintain or grow his distinguished status.

Simile

Which of these is an example of simile in the passage?

A   *Sweat on my forehead rushes like a river to my eyes.*

B   *It slips from my hands as though they were buttered.*

C   *There's no such thing as a fumble in baseball.*

D   *As we head to the locker room, I keep admiring that baseball in my still-stinging hands.*

Correct answer: A

Strategies

✓ *Recognize the item type and know common literary techniques well.*

This item asks students to identify an example of the literary technique *simile*. By definition, a simile is a comparison between two or more things using the words *like* or *as*. Students must know and apply the definition of *simile*; otherwise they will have little chance of answering this item correctly.

✓ *Have an anchor example.*

In this identification item, students can use an anchor example to their advantage. For instance, students can find a memorable example from the collection of poems *Come With Me: Poems for a Journey* (see the activity on page 162). Students might choose *a sleep as deep as desert sand* as an

example of simile that they can keep in their mind. Then these students will be able to use it to recall that a simile is a comparison (that is, the depth of sleep is compared to the depth of desert sand) that uses the word *as*. (If students' simile example using *as* does not help them recall that both *like* and *as* can be used to form similes, then students should memorize an additional example that uses *like*.)

✓ *Focus on the comparison.*

Unfortunately, in this identification item, students cannot simply search for the option that contains the word *like* or *as*. Students should then recognize that the correct answer will be the option that presents a comparison. To find the comparison, students can ask two key questions:

1. What two things are being compared?
2. What is the writer saying that these two things have in common?

Essentially, students are looking for two nouns or subjects. A simple graphic can help students try to isolate two nouns and think about whether a comparison is made. Figure 6.1 shows how option A works with the graphic.

Students should be able to determine that sweat and a river are both made of water and that the author is making this comparison to emphasize how much Jake is sweating.

The sentences in options B, C, and D do not present comparisons.

FIGURE 6.1 **Finding a Comparison in a Simile**

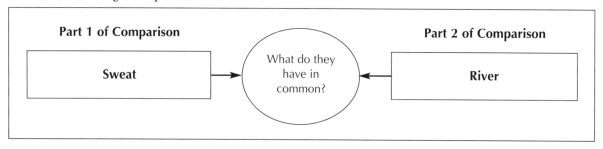

Metaphor

In paragraph 1, the author uses the metaphor "The Texas heat is the enemy" to—

A   establish the setting of the story
B   reflect the narrator's fear of playing sports
C   state the central conflict of the story
D   express the narrator's feelings about his surroundings

Correct answer: D

Strategies

✓ *Locate important information in the item.*

The item stem tells students the following:

- What sentence (metaphor) is being tested (*The Texas heat is the enemy*)
- Where the sentence is located in the passage (paragraph 1).

✓ *Recognize the item type.*

In this item, students are explicitly told in the stem that the tested sentence is a metaphor. The words *the author uses* tells students that they are expected to analyze the intended effect of the metaphor.

✓ *Know common literary techniques well.*

Technically, metaphors come in many forms. Metaphors can be idioms, personification, and language use in which the intended meaning is metaphoric or figurative rather than literal. Often, though, standardized assessments test metaphor as a comparison stated directly (as opposed to a simile that uses the words *like* or *as*).

In this item, students are aided by the word *metaphor* in the stem. Students need to know common literary techniques well enough to understand that metaphors are direct comparisons. The stem points students to paragraph 1, in which the metaphor appears, because the context is important in deriving the interpretive meaning of the metaphor. Why the heat in Texas is compared to an enemy is not immediately clear without consideration of other plot events.

✓ *Have an anchor example.*

Students who recognize this item as testing metaphor can use an anchor example of metaphor to their advantage. The activity on pages 163–164 allows students to create a memorable example of metaphor. Students who recall their example of metaphor (such as "I am a walking encyclopedia") can use it to recognize that a metaphor is a comparison (*I* is compared to an *encyclopedia*).

✓ *Ask key questions.*

Once students recall their knowledge of metaphor, they can ask themselves two questions to focus on the comparison's meaning:

1. What is being compared?
2. What is the writer saying that these two things have in common?

As noted earlier, students should return to the passage to find context clues that support the interpretive meaning of the metaphor. To do so, students must isolate the two things being compared; they might visualize that information as shown in Figure 6.2.

While simple, the graphic reminds students to ponder how the Texas heat can be compared to, or can be considered similar to, an enemy of Jake. Students should think of the qualities of an enemy in a literal sense in order to know why the author uses the image in a figurative way. Students might say that an enemy is something that is against another person or is someone who makes things hard for another person. This is the right frame of mind as students consider each of the four options.

FIGURE 6.2 **Finding a Comparison in a Metaphor**

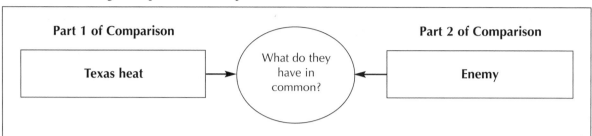

✓ *Build a case.*

As a result of being urged by the item stem to reread paragraph 1, students are likely to pick out details that relate to the comparison. They might focus on *every day is the same* and *unnoticed* and the fact that Jake doesn't think he will need to wear his glove in order to conclude that he finds gym class to be a humdrum experience—imprisoning, actually. These details are the support that is needed to make the case that option D, "express the narrator's feelings about his surroundings," is the correct answer.

But because the options speak to the author's intention and sound like important ideas, students should try to build a case for the other options as well; only then can they be certain that little evidence for the incorrect options can be accumulated.

Option A, "establish the setting," will likely be quite appealing to students. After all, the sentence does state where the story takes place—Texas. Students have to consider whether an author would use a metaphor to establish the setting or if literary techniques like metaphors are used for more important reasons. In this case, the metaphor tells us more about Jake's feelings about his situation than it describes where Jake is; it establishes an atmosphere more than it establishes a setting. The setting is Jake's gym class, on a baseball field, amongst his peers; because other sentences in paragraph 1 do a much better job of establishing the setting than the metaphor, this option is not correct.

Students should be hard pressed to find information in the passage that supports option B, "reflect the narrator's fear of playing sports." Students might find this option appealing only if they think about other details in paragraph 1 rather than the metaphor. However, there is no literal mention of fear in the plot. It should be clear to students that Jake is miserable, but he is not particularly fearful. Therefore, there is no evidence that the author mentions the heat of the day in order to make readers think that Jake is fearful of playing sports—that doesn't make much sense at all.

Option C, "state the central conflict of the story," seems less far-fetched than option B. Because the word *enemy* appears in the metaphor, students might initially try to make a connection between *enemy* and *central conflict*. But when students recall the details of paragraph 1, they should determine that Jake's problem is not that he's hot—it's that he is in gym class and hates it. Therefore, the author establishes the conflict in paragraph 1, but not through the use of a metaphor.

Trying to build a case for each option reveals that only option D can be supported fully and is therefore the correct answer.

Personification

Which of these is an example of personification in the passage?

A *Rubbing them doesn't lessen the stinging . . .*

B *. . . the sun punishes us with blinding rays . . .*

C *. . . only because the teacher is watching.*

D *I hit the ground hard.*

Correct answer: B

Strategies

✓ *Recognize the item type and know common literary techniques well.*

Students must apply the definition of *personification*—giving human qualities to nonhuman things—in order to identify an example of it.

✓ *Have an anchor example.*

In this identification item, students can use an anchor example of personification to their advantage. The activity on pages 164–165 allows students to create a memorable example (such as "The stars refused to show up for work last night") that they can recall to help them during a reading assessment.

✓ *Find the noun and find the verb.*

In this item, the options are actual phrases lifted from the passage. Because personification hinges on giving human qualities (usually a verb) to nonhuman things (usually a noun or the subject), it is rare for personification to exist without a noun and a verb. (Personification can also be created with an adjective and a noun, as in *whispering wind,* but these examples are more infrequent in literature than a noun-verb combination.)

A marking system can focus students' attention on the noun and the verb in each option, as illustrated here, where the nouns are in parentheses and the verbs are underlined:

A (Rubbing them [eyes]) <u>doesn't lessen</u> the stinging . . .

B . . . (sun) <u>punishes</u> us with blinding rays . . .

C . . . only because the (teacher) <u>is watching</u>.

D (I) <u>hit</u> the ground hard.

By isolating the nouns and verbs in the options, students can begin to rule out the options that do not fit the definition of personification—ascribing something human (verb) to something nonhuman (noun).

If isolating the subject and the verb fails to reveal an example of personification, students should isolate the subject (which will be the nonhuman thing) and look for other parts of speech that indicate a human quality, such as adjectives (as in the example *whispering wind*).

✓ *Find something human and nonhuman.*

Pose questions about whether the noun/subject refers to something nonhuman and the verb to something human:

A Are (eyes) nonhuman? Do humans <u>lessen</u>?

B Is a (sun) nonhuman? Do humans <u>punish others</u>?

C Is (a teacher) nonhuman? Is <u>to watch something</u> human?

D Is (I) nonhuman? Is <u>hit</u> human?

Only option B answers both the questions affirmatively. Therefore, the phrase *the sun punishes us* is an example of attributing a human characteristic (punishment) to a nonhuman thing (the sun).

✓ *Ask a key question.*

Personification has a figurative meaning, not a literal one. Students can check their answer by making sure the example is not literal in meaning. They can ask themselves, "Did that *literally* happen?" Students should immediately recognize that, for option B, the sun was intense, but it didn't *literally* punish Jake.

Hyperbole

Which sentence from the passage contains an example of hyperbole?

  A   *The nearest opponent is three city blocks away.*

  B   *I glance at Paul, and neither he nor I can believe I have caught it.*

  C   *As we head to the locker room, I keep admiring that baseball in my still-stinging hands.*

  D   *I figure one fewer ball in the equipment locker won't matter.*

Correct answer: A

Strategies

✓ *Recognize the item type and know common literary techniques well.*

Students must apply the definition of *hyperbole*—exaggeration (simply put)—in order to identify an example of it.

✓ *Have an anchor example.*

Students who can access an anchor example of hyperbole during a reading assessment may be able to make short work of this identification item. The activity on pages 165–166 presents students with a number of examples from which students can choose or create their own.

✓ *Go from "tall talk" to "plain talk."*

Because hyperbole is exaggeration, students need to determine which of the four options embellishes an idea rather than states a literal idea. They might think in terms of trying to "translate" the options from something that is an overstatement of the truth to something that expresses the idea in more ordinary terms. The simple structure that follows shows how option A can be translated.

Overstatement	→	More Accurate Statement
The nearest opponent is three city blocks away.		*The nearest opponent is far away.*

The other options cannot be translated from overstatement to accurate statement. Options B, C, and D already represent actual, realistic, literal events or details in the passage. That is, Paul literally cannot believe that Jake has caught the ball (option B); Jake literally admires the ball in his hands while he walks to the locker room (option C); Jake literally thinks that it won't matter if he doesn't put the ball in the equipment locker (option D).

✓ *Identify and explain the exaggeration.*

A variant on the previous strategy is for students to (1) identify the words in the statement that provide the exaggeration, and (2) explain why those particular words signal exaggeration.

In option A, the words that provide the exaggeration are *three city blocks away*. Students should be able to explain that an opponent must be present on the football field, so this person cannot be three city blocks away. Further, students should be able to recognize that the author uses hyperbole in this sentence to help readers understand that Jake knows that the other players do not consider him a threat and that is why no one is guarding him.

Analogy

At the end of paragraph 1, the author uses an analogy to express the narrator's—

A desire to be accepted
B familiarity with ordinary experiences
C anticipation of the end of gym class
D lack of self-control

Correct answer: C

Strategies

✓ *Recognize the item type and know common literary techniques well.*

The word *analogy* in the item stem clearly indicates to students what this item is assessing. An analogy is a comparison between two dissimilar things, usually to make a point or create an image.

In this item, because the analogy itself is not identified, students must first apply a definition of the term and then interpret what the analogy reveals about the narrator.

✓ *Find out what two things are being compared.*

Even though the item stem indicates that the analogy appears at the end of the paragraph, students should reread all of paragraph 1 to gain the context.

Then students should analyze each sentence toward the end of the paragraph to determine if two dissimilar things are being compared. Students should recognize that the analogy is presented in the sentence "I wait for class to be over the way a prisoner waits to be released"; here, the narrator compares himself to a prisoner.

✓ *Relate what you know to what you don't know.*

Authors use analogies to help readers use information that they *do know* to help them understand something new or something they *don't know*. In this case, the author wants readers to relate their knowledge of a prisoner's experience (something they can speculate about) to help them understand Jake's experience (someone they don't know).

To understand the analogy at the end of paragraph 1, students should call up what they can about a prisoner's experience and then determine if Jake's experience is parallel, as shown in Figure 6.3.

By relating a prisoner's experience to Jake's, the correct answer essentially reveals itself—Jake wants to be freed from his experience in gym class, just as a prisoner desires freedom.

FIGURE 6.3 **Comparison of a Prisoner to Jake**

A Prisoner	Jake
• Is likely miserable	• Says he is miserable
• Has no freedom	• Is required to take gym class
• Probably looks forward to being released	• Probably wants gym class to be over

Flashback

Which words signal the beginning of a flashback?

A   *A baseball is indeed heading toward me . . .*

B   *. . . I am transported back to the fourth grade.*

C   *That's when Paul does the unthinkable.*

D   *As we head to the locker room . . .*

Correct answer: B

FIGURE 6.4   **Shifts in Setting**

	Place	**Time**
Paragraphs 1–2	Baseball field	Eighth grade
Paragraphs 3–5	Playground	Fourth grade
Paragraphs 6–7	Baseball field	Eighth grade
Paragraphs 8–10	Locker room	Eighth grade
Paragraph 11	Math class	Eighth grade
Paragraph 12	Baseball field	Eighth grade

Strategies

✓ *Recognize the item type and know common literary techniques.*

The word *flashback* in the item stem clearly identifies what this item is testing. Flashback is the device used by an author to insert a scene from the past into the present chronological structure of a literary text. In this item, students are told in the item stem that a flashback exists in the passage and are asked to identify the words the author uses as a signal.

✓ *Find a major shift in time.*

Setting is the place and time in a story. Within a story, the action can happen in several different places. So looking for a shift in place is not necessarily an indication of flashback.

A shift in time is a better indicator of flashback. After all, stories told chronologically usually present a set of events that happen fairly close together in time. That is not the case in this passage. The author purposefully takes the reader back in time to an earlier event that is significant. Going from middle school back to elementary school is a significant shift in time.

Therefore, knowing the settings in a passage is key to identifying flashback, but only if students consider place *and* time, as shown in Figure 6.4.

Many shifts in place exist, but only one significant shift back in time exists and thus tells students when the flashback begins; this makes option B the clear answer.

✓ *Ask a key question.*

A flashback is a choice that an author makes because he or she wants to make readers aware of an earlier event that impacts or better explains present events. It is as though the author is saying, with a wink, "Let me fill you in." On middle school assessments, flashback items may move beyond simple identification and ask students about the purpose of a flashback:

The author includes a flashback in order to—
A   explain Jake's attitude about playing sports
B   compare two sports
C   reveal how Jake feels about being outdoors
D   contrast elementary school with middle school

(The correct answer is option A.)

For flashback questions requiring analysis, such as this one, students can ask themselves this key question: "How does knowing this past event help me understand these present events more completely?" The answer is option A because the purpose of the flashback is to let readers in on an embarrassing experience from the past to explain why Jake is so miserable on the sports field. In other words, Jake's fourth-grade embarrassment explains his eighth-grade trepidation!

Foreshadowing

What does the title of the passage foreshadow?

A   The words the coach says to Jake
B   The feeling Jake has on the football field
C   The way Jake feels about playing sports
D   The reaction Jake receives from his baseball teammates

Correct answer: D

Strategies

✓ *Recognize the item type.*

The word *foreshadow* tells students that this item assesses foreshadowing. Instead of using the word *foreshadow*, an item might use the word *clue* or *hint*, as in "Which detail at the beginning of the story provides a hint about what happens later?"

✓ *Know common literary techniques well.*

Foreshadowing refers to the clues or hints an author uses to indicate to the reader what will happen later in the story.

Oftentimes, students do not pick up on foreshadowing as they are reading but can recognize the clue *after* they have finished the story. That is, on a reading test, students might not realize that foreshadowing exists in a story until they are made aware of it by the existence of a foreshadowing item! Fortunately, it doesn't matter when or how students notice the foreshadowing as long as they are able to recognize why the author embedded it.

✓ *Ask a key question.*

In this item, students have to first analyze the title to realize that someone in the story changes from feeling like a nobody to feeling like a somebody.

Then, because foreshadowing helps the reader know something now about something that will occur later, students can use this basic definition to question the options, as shown here:

A   Does knowing the title "The Gym Class ~~Nobody~~ Somebody" now help me know something later about the coach's words? (*No.*)
B   Does knowing the title "The Gym Class ~~Nobody~~ Somebody" now help me know something later about Jake's feelings on the football field? (*No.*)
C   Does knowing the title "The Gym Class ~~Nobody~~ Somebody" now help me know something later about Jake's feelings playing sports? (*No.*)
D   Does knowing the title "The Gym Class ~~Nobody~~ Somebody" now help me know something later about Jake's reaction to his baseball teammates? (*Yes. Because of the positive reaction that Jake receives after catching the baseball, he feels like a* somebody *rather than a* nobody.)

The emphasis on how information early on provides information about an event later on is critical in order for students to detect foreshadowing. This frame of mind should help students recognize that only option D can be the answer.

Symbolism

Jake wants to keep the baseball most likely because it represents—

A   gaining recognition from his peers
B   exploring new interests
C   receiving help from others
D   accepting himself as he is

Correct answer: A

Strategies

✓ *Recognize the item type and know common literary techniques well.*

The key word in the item stem is *represents*. The words *symbol(izes), signifies,* and *stands for* can also be used in symbolism items.

Symbols are places, people, or things/objects that represent something else (or something greater). In this item, students are asked to analyze what the baseball means to Jake. Oftentimes, students are asked to uncover how a concrete object (in this case, a baseball) is a symbol of something more abstract (such as a feeling or sentiment).

✓ *Look for change—or not!*

Sometimes a symbol takes on meaning because it is connected to a change in a character's circumstances. In this passage, that is certainly the case: Catching the baseball puts the spotlight on Jake for a moment and causes his change in attitude about gym class. Jake asks to keep the baseball because it means something to him.

Other times a symbol is meaningful because it is connected to something that never changes. An example might be family traditions or landmarks that are special to a character; they can be counted on because they stay the same.

✓ *Look for a cause-effect relationship that makes sense.*

One way to conceptualize the connection between the object (the baseball) and its meaning to Jake is to formulate a cause-effect relationship with each option and then assess the relationship's validity, as shown here:

A Jake keeps the baseball *because* he gains his peers' recognition. (*Yes.*)
B Jake keeps the baseball *because* he explores a new interest. (*No.*)
C Jake keeps the baseball *because* he receives help from others. (*No.*)
D Jake keeps the baseball *because* he accepts himself as he is. (*No.*)

Phrasing option A in this way highlights that Jake's catching the baseball makes him visible again to his teammates; he wants to keep the baseball as a reminder of that moment. Option A makes perfect sense.

The other options should seem less attractive than they might have when students first read the item. That is, initially, students might think that a few of the options make some sense; after all, Jake does appear to be interested in baseball in the last paragraph (option B), and his self-image does improve (option D). But when the options are phrased as cause-effect relationships, students should clearly see that Jake does not keep the ball because he has a new interest or receives help or accepts himself as he is. Only option A correctly expresses the significance of the baseball to Jake.

✓ *Think about what would be missing.*

Another option for determining a symbol's significance is to think about what would be missing from the character's story without the place, person, or thing/object that serves as a symbol.

Students should realize that before catching the ball, Jake is miserable in gym class and feels invisible. But after catching the ball, Jake receives heaping praise—this is the part of the story that would be missing. So students should reason that Jake wants to keep the baseball because it symbolizes attention, or, as option A is worded, recognition from his peers.

Mood and Tone

The mood in paragraphs 7 through 11 is best described as—

A peaceful

B serious

C relaxed

D celebratory

Correct answer: D

Strategies

✔ *Recognize the item type.*

The word *mood* in the stem clearly indicates that this item tests students' understanding of mood. Tone items can be structured in the same way. Mood and tone items might also use the words *sense of, atmosphere,* and *feeling.*

✔ *Know common literary techniques well.*

Mood and tone can be confusing to students. Mood is the atmosphere or state of mind that the reader experiences while reading. Tone is the author's attitude about the subject or the approach/style of writing that is used (such as objective or critical). A (reductionistic) way to conceptualize these literary techniques is to think "How the reader feels is the mood; how the author feels is the tone."

To uncover the mood of the specified paragraphs, students should imagine filming the scene with a camera. As students picture what is happening, they should consider the feeling they get from the action and the characters' words and emotions.

In paragraphs 7 through 11, students would need to capture Jake's feelings of joy and pride after catching the baseball. Jake is caught rather off guard by his teammates' reactions of pure excitement. The situation is far from serious (option B). The cheering means that the scene is not peaceful (option A) or relaxed (option C). It is a time for celebration (option D).

✔ *Study the words the author uses.*

How do authors create an atmosphere? With words. Focusing on the words the author uses to relate events to readers will reveal the mood.

By combing through paragraphs 7 through 11, students can pull out words and phrases that support each mood presented as an answer choice, as shown in Figure 6.5.

This strategy—called "building a case" elsewhere—helps students see that only option D is well supported by the text. In fact, students should have to "reach" to find any evidence at all to support the other answer choices, as demonstrated below with the tentative examples of "Maybe: . . ." Option D is clearly the answer.

✔ *Picture the scene.*

Figure 6.5 Text Support for Each Mood

A peaceful	None, really. Maybe: *As we head to the locker room, I keep admiring that baseball in my still-stinging hands.*	
B serious	None, really. Maybe: *I look down at the mound in the metal ball basket.*	
C relaxed	None, really. Maybe: *I smile, too, pocketing my ball proudly.*	
D celebratory	*"Way to go, Jake," is the first cheer I hear.* *There are others—lots of them.* *As we head to the locker room, I keep admiring that baseball in my still-stinging hands.* *"Nice catch," he says.* *But that ball does matter to me. A lot.* *. . . flashing a knowing smile and patting me on the back.* *I smile, too, pocketing my ball proudly.* *For the rest of the day, my gloveless catch is big news.* *In math class, instead of doing their work, the guys entertain some girls by recounting the moment in a dramatic sportscaster's voice.*	

Style

In the last paragraph, what does the author do to slow down the action?

A   Switches tense and speaks directly to readers

B   Uses persuasive language and credible evidence

C   Shifts the point of view from first to third person

D   Uses language that appeals to the senses

Correct answer: A

Strategies

✓ *Recognize the item type.*

Items assessing an author's style can be difficult to detect for students by the stem alone, usually because the word *style* is not used. In order to recognize what this item is assessing, students have to recognize that trying to *slow down the action* of prose has to do with an author's style or craft. Furthermore, students could benefit from reading the answer choices and recognizing that the author's use of tense, language, and point of view are all stylistic decisions.

✓ *Know common literary techniques well.*

Items about style can cover a number of issues, from *how* an author achieves an effect to *why* an author would want to achieve a certain effect. Students might be asked about the author's use of dialogue, dialect, and sound devices. Students might be asked about the construction of sentences, such as the effect of using a sentence fragment or repeating words. Students might be asked about the way the author introduces a topic (especially in informational passages). The activity on pages 169–170 provides examples of an author's use of style and should help get students noticing how and why an author presents information.

✓ *Ask a key question (or four).*

This item essentially asks students to identify what the author is doing stylistically in the last paragraph. To give the item rigor, the options are composed of style choices an author *might* make; only one of the options, however, is a choice the author *did* make and is therefore the correct answer. Students can form questions about the style choices presented as the four options to determine which option is supported, as shown in Figure 6.6.

FIGURE 6.6   **Questions and Evidence About Style Choices**

Options	Questions	Evidence
Switches tense and speaks directly to readers	Does the author switch from present to past or past to present?	*Yes. The author uses past tense in the last paragraph.*
	Does the author speak directly to the reader?	*Yes. The author uses* you *in the first sentence of the last paragraph.*
Uses persuasive language and credible evidence	Does the author take a stand on an issue and use facts and statistics?	*No.*
Shifts the point of view from first person to third person	Does the author stop using *I* and start using *he/she* or *they*?	*No.*
Uses language that appeals to the senses	Does the author use description that emphasizes the five senses?	*No.*

Because students can find evidence to support option A, they should be able to recognize that the author changes the tense and speaks directly to the reader in order to bring the story to a screeching halt. Paragraph 11 is a high point for Jake—his catch is big news—and in paragraph 12, he is picked last—a low point for Jake, at least temporarily. These important events stick out to the reader because of the choices the author makes stylistically in order to slow the pace. Only option A is supported.

Chapter 7

Interpretations

This chapter presents information about the most common types of items used to assess interpretations on state assessments—those that typically require critical thinking. These include cause-effect, chronology, conclusion/inference, comparison/contrast, fact/opinion, prediction, and supporting evidence. The following are examples, not particular to any state, of reading standards for interpretations. Students are expected to do the following:

- In inferred *cause-effect relationships*, recognize a cause for an effect and an effect for a cause
- Place events in *chronological* (time order) *sequence*
- Use evidence from the passage to draw a *conclusion* or make an *inference*
- Compare and *contrast* information across one or more texts
- Distinguish *fact* from *opinion*
- Make a reasonable *prediction* based on information in the passage
- *Support* an assertion or conclusion with textual *evidence*

Basic Strategies for Interpretations Items

The following basic strategies are good starting points for teachers to share with students as they work together to make sense of reading test items about interpretations. Later in this chapter, strategies that are specific to certain types of interpretations items are explored.

✓ *Recognize the item type.*

Cause-effect. There is usually at least one recognizable clue in the stem of an item testing cause-effect. The words *cause, effect, why, because, result*, or *outcome* in the stem tell students to think about a relationship between two events.

The distractors for a cause-effect item can be true events from the passage or they can be misrepresented events; either way, the distractors will be wrong because they do not have a direct relationship to the event specified in the item stem.

Chronology. There is usually at least one recognizable clue in the stem of an item testing chronology. The words *which event occurs* or *what happens* indicate to students that they should think about text chronology, as do the words *before, after, first*, and *last*.

Typically, the options for a chronology item will be true events from the passage, accurately represented. Students do not have the advantage of trying to determine if any option does not appear in the passage and is therefore not viable. So, students really have to focus on the relationship that is being established between the event featured in the stem and the one correct answer. Furthermore, students must realize that chronology items ask where an event appears in time, which might be complicated by an author's use of flashback or inferences readers might need to make about events that are implied or otherwise unseen in the passage.

Conclusion/inference. Conclusion/inference items test students' ability to take what the author tells them explicitly and draw reasonable conclusions or make reasonable inferences about that information. Such items require high-level thinking and can be difficult for students. The words *based on* and words such as *tell, conclude*, and *infer* are signals to students that they cannot simply point to the answer in the passage.

Comparison/Contrast. Comparison/contrast items test students' ability to make connections across text. The words *similar, alike, common*, and *different* are the most common signals to students that they have to think about two or more ideas or concepts presented in the passage. Comparison/contrast items can be posed for two or more ideas within a single passage (as is the case in the sample item that is presented later in the chapter) or can be posed about an idea in paired passages (see Section 3 for examples).

Fact/opinion. Identifying items that test opinions is easy for students, because the word *opinion* will appear in the stems. For items testing facts, the word *fact* will appear. Usually, there is little variation on the phrasing of fact/opinion items. In informational passages, readers may have to read closely, because an author's opinion might be presented as fact or may be so closely woven with facts that students might not initially recognize that the author has inserted himself or herself into the text. Fact/opinion items are much less frequently tested in literary passages, but for the sake of illustration, one item is included in this section; the strategies presented apply equally as well to fact/opinion items about informational texts.

Prediction. While there are a number of ways to phrase prediction items, students are provided with clue words in the stems to indicate that the items test prediction; otherwise, students will not know that they have to think beyond the boundaries of the passage. These clue words include *will happen next, after the story ends, the reader can predict that, if the story had continued,* and *in the future.*

Supporting evidence. The structure of supporting evidence items is usually the same: Students are provided with a conclusion or an important idea in the stem, such as a character trait or theme, and are asked to select, among four quoted sentences or four paraphrased ideas, the information that best supports the idea presented in the stem. The quoted text can come from one paragraph or from various paragraphs. The options might be ordered according to how they appear in the passage or they might be scrambled. The options might or might not be set off in a special way—such as with italics—to indicate that they are lifted from the passage.

✓ *Locate the options in the passage.*

For items that assess *literal* understandings, such as those testing details, it makes perfect sense to track down the options in the passage in order to be able to point to the answer—after all, the answer is often stated *literally* in the passage.

But it's also important to track down the options in the passage for other types of items—even those requiring *interpretations*. The options for many types of interpretation items are true events (or true information) from the passage. So, simply knowing where the events (that the options describe) appear in the passage can offer clues about the answers to various interpretation items. Take cause-effect relationships, for instance. In the typical structure of a text, usually a cause precedes an effect; the author presents a cause and effect in close proximity so that readers will recognize that a relationship exists. Therefore, students who track down the events in the item stem and options and find that two exist reasonably close together are provided with a hint that a cause-effect relationship might exist between them.

As another example, chronology items ask students to juggle *five* events at once—the event provided in the item stem and the event presented in each of the four options. In order to keep the events from muddling in their minds, students should take a moment to find each event in the passage and make note of it. Often the answer to a chronology item reveals itself to students while they are in the process of tracking down the options. If not, students can use other clues—such as settings—to make sense of which events precede or follow others.

Encouraging students to return to the passage to track down events and important information—even with items that require interpretations—can

FIGURE 7.1
Item Types and
Key Questions

Item Types	Key Questions
Cause-effect	Does [this] lead to [that]?
Chronology	Does [this] precede/follow [that]?
Conclusion/inference	What does the passage say about [this]?
Prediction	Can readers know [this]?

build their understanding that the answers to items lie somewhere within the text itself, sometimes literally stated and sometimes bubbling just beneath the surface.

✓ *Ask a key question.*

"Ask a key question" is a strategy that has been sprinkled into previous chapters for certain types of items. In essence, this strategy in its many forms helps students get to the heart of certain definitions and features that compose certain types of items. Examples of some of the key questions students can ask themselves for the standards in this chapter are shown in Figure 7.1.

Posing questions in this way requires students to think about the core of a particular reading standard. In many ways, key questions set students on the necessary path toward determining the correct answer.

✓ *Build a case.*

"Build a case" is yet another strategy that has been sprinkled into previous chapters for certain types of items. If the strategy's name sounds a bit like something a lawyer would do, that's the intent. Building a case for the options of an item is a strategy that asks students to think through each one and to formulate reasons and find evidence that make an option either correct or incorrect. While building a case is another way of saying "support the answer" and can be applied to many types of items, the strategy is especially helpful to use with items about interpretations.

Cause-Effect

The author implies that Jake keeps the baseball he catches because—

A   he forgets to place it in the equipment locker
B   Coach Wilson understands the ball's significance to him
C   he wants to show it to the girls in math class
D   Coach Wilson wants him to practice playing baseball at home

Correct answer: B

Strategies

✓ Recognize the item type.

The word *because* tells students that they should think about a cause-effect relationship. In addition, the word *implies* indicates that the cause-effect relationship is implied rather than stated literally.

The options for this cause-effect item are true events from the passage, so students must determine which three are wrong because they do not have a direct relationship to the event specified in the item stem.

Alternate versions of cause-effect items are presented in Figure 7.2.

FIGURE 7.2   **Alternate Versions of Cause-Effect Items**

> Jake is able to keep the baseball he catches most likely *because*—
>
> What *causes* Jake to feel embarrassed on the football field?
>
> *Why* is Jake the subject among his peers in math class?
>
> What is the *effect* of Jake's catching the baseball?
>
> *As a result* of talking to Coach Wilson, Jake—
>
> What is an important *outcome* of Jake's catching the baseball?

FIGURE 7.3   **Visualizing a Cause-Effect Relationship**

Cause	⟶	Effect
?	⟶	Jake keeps the baseball.

✓ Figure out which part of the cause-effect relationship is provided.

In a cause-effect relationship item, the cause can be provided and students must recognize the effect, or the effect can be provided and students must recognize the cause. When the stem does not use the word *cause* or *effect*, it might be difficult initially for students to understand which part of a cause-effect relationship they are searching for. Students can use the key word *because* to know that they are looking for the cause and that the stem provides the effect. Visualizing the relationship in graphic form, as shown in Figure 7.3, can help.

✓ Ask a key question.

Sometimes when a cause-effect item provides the effect in the stem and asks for the cause, students can become confused because the information feels "backward." Posing the relationship as a question can help test the sense of each option:

A   Does *forgetting to place the ball in the locker* CAUSE Jake to keep the baseball? (*No.*)
B   Does *Coach Wilson understand that the ball has significance to Jake and that is what* CAUSES Jake to keep the baseball? (*Yes.*)
C   Does *wanting to show off the ball to some girls* CAUSE Jake to keep the baseball? (*No.*)
D   Does *Coach Wilson want Jake to practice more and that is what* CAUSES Jake to keep the baseball? (*No.*)

Only option B presents an event that takes place in the story. Read together, the item stem and option B form a clear cause-effect relationship that is true of the events that take place in paragraphs 8 through 10.

✓ *Build a case.*

This item requires interpretation since the stem clearly indicates that the cause-effect relationship is implied. Therefore, students should be able to mount evidence that would lead readers to make the correct interpretation.

To support option B, students should be able to put together the information that after Jake asks whether he can keep the baseball (paragraph 9), the coach says, "No problem" (paragraph 10). Then details in paragraph 10 help the reader know why: the coach flashes "a knowing smile" and pats Jake on the back. These details help readers understand that the coach knows that Jake wants to keep the baseball because it means something to him (paragraph 9), which is why Jake pockets the ball proudly (paragraph 10).

Chronology

What happens right after Paul throws the ball to Jake?

   A   Jake fumbles the ball.
   B   Jake hears his teammates' shouts.
   C   Jake runs to try to make a touchdown.
   D   Jake asks his coach if he can keep the ball.

Correct answer: C

Strategies

✔ *Recognize the item type.*

The words *what happens right after* tell students that they should think about the text's chronology.

Alternate versions of chronology items are presented in Figure 7.4.

✔ *Locate the event in the stem and options in the passage.*

Chronology items can appear quite easy on the surface, causing students to think that they can remember the passage events sufficiently well enough to answer the item without turning back to reread. But chronology items, such as this one, can be deceptively simple because the answer seems obvious: After Paul throws the ball to Jake, Jake does fumble it. Correct? Well, while it is true that Jake fumbles the ball, it is not the event that happens *right after* Paul throws the ball to him.

Returning to the passage to locate the events and putting the paragraph reference next to each option is a good first step to recalling when the events happened:

FIGURE 7.4 **Alternate Versions of Chronology Items**

Which event happened *first* in the story?
Which of these events happened *last*?
What must happen *before* _____?
When _____ goes to do _____, what happens?

What happens right after Paul throws the ball to Jake? (beginning of paragraph 5)

   A Jake fumbles the ball. (end of paragraph 5)
   B Jake hears his teammates' shouts. (end of paragraph 2)
   C Jake runs to try to make a touchdown. (middle of paragraph 5)
   D Jake asks his coach if he can keep the ball. (middle of paragraph 9)

The specific locations of the events within the paragraphs provide students with a fairly good idea about the most viable options. That is, the event that happens right after another event is likely to appear in the same paragraph or the next paragraph. So, because options A and C are events that happen in paragraph 5—just as the event in the stem does—these two options look the most promising. Options B and D can likely be eliminated.

Students can then use any of the strategies that follow to think about the time order of the events rather than simply their location in the passage.

✔ *Use a graphic organizer to think about time order.*

Putting the events on a time line or in sequenced boxes helps students to think about time order. After students make note of paragraph references for each option, they can confirm whether the plot makes sense if the events are ordered according to where they appear in the passage, as shown in Figure 7.5.

By using a time line, students can see that options B and D do not belong on the time line because they present events that happen significantly later in time—in middle school rather than in elementary school. Of options A and C, the event in option C—Jake runs to make a touchdown—is the one that happens right after the event in the stem—Paul throws the ball to Jake.

FIGURE 7.5 **Time Line of Plot Events**

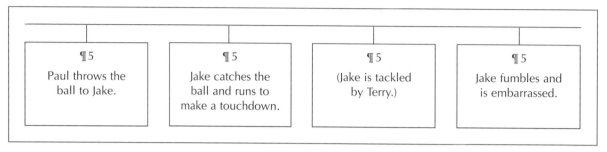

It is important for students to understand that a chronology item isn't simply asking where the event appears in the passage, but rather when the event occurs in time. In this item, for instance, even though option B occurs *first* in the passage, it actually is an event that occurs *after* the event in the stem. Students will likely need exposure to items like this one so that they understand the importance of thinking about the events based on time order rather than passage placement.

✓ *Group events by setting.*
Another strategy for accounting for shifts in time in passages is to record the events by time (for example, eighth grade, fourth grade, back to eighth grade) or by place (for example, middle school gym class/baseball field, elementary school playground, middle school math class). Using this strategy, students should realize that an event that happens at another time is not one that could happen "right after" any other event:

What happens right after Paul throws the ball to Jake?

A Jake fumbles the ball. (same day)
B Jake hears his teammates' shouts. (different day)
C Jake runs to try to make a touchdown. (same day)
D Jake asks his coach if he can keep the ball. (different day)

Options A and C happen the same day as the event in the stem and are therefore viable because one of them is likely to have happened "right after." Students can feel confident about ruling out options B and D because they happen much later in time.

Or, students can also track events by setting:

What happens right after Paul throws the ball to Jake? (on playground)

A Jake fumbles the ball. (on playground)
B Jake hears his teammates' shouts. (on baseball field)
C Jake runs to try to make a touchdown. (on playground)
D Jake asks his coach if he can keep the ball. (on baseball field)

Again, only options A and C happen in the same location as the event provided in the stem—and it makes sense, then, that one would happen right after another. Students can feel confident about dismissing these two options based on this strategy.

It is important that students have multiple, easy-to-use strategies when approaching chronology items, because some strategies will be more effective for eliminating options than others. For this sample item, the record-events-by-time and record-events-by-place strategies help students eliminate only two of the three wrong options, whereas the time line strategy helps students eliminate all three of the wrong answer choices.

Conclusion/Inference

What can the reader conclude from the team-mates' comments in paragraph 2?

A   They think of Jake as an important member of the team.

B   They are not confident that Jake will make the catch.

C   They don't understand why Jake isn't wearing his glove.

D   They know the blinding sun is distracting to Jake.

Correct answer: B

Strategies

✓ *Recognize the item type.*

The word *conclude* indicates that this item requires students to draw a conclusion or make an inference; in other words, the answer is not stated in the passage. Other signal words include *tell, infer, assume, likely, probably,* and *based on information in the passage.*

✓ *Use information in the item stem as a clue to important information in the passage.*

Most conclusion/inference items ask about an important event in the passage, requiring students to pinpoint the general area in which the answer can be surmised or directing students to a particular part of the passage in which the answer can be interpreted (as is the case with this item).

As students reread paragraph 2, they should focus on mentions of the teammates' comments, as indicated in the item stem, in order to form an interpretation of what Jake's teammates say to him:

"<u>Get under it</u>, Jake," someone <u>commands</u>.
"<u>Don't be scared</u> of it," someone else <u>hollers</u>.

As shown here with the underlining, students can examine what the teammates say as well as the verbs the author uses to describe how the team-mates are saying these words; both provide clues about the correct answer. The teammates are instructing Jake about what to do, and they are doing so insistently. Of the four options, option B seems to be the most viable answer.

✓ *Build a case.*

Students can focus on key textual evidence by trying to build a case for each option. Doing so will help students develop an understanding that drawing conclusions and inferences is about stepping away from what the passage literally says to thinking about what those words actually mean. A key question for building a case for each option is, "What does the passage say about . . . ?" which can be adjusted for this sample item to be, "What does paragraph 2 say about . . . ?" as shown in Figure 7.6.

By trying to build a case for each option, students should be able to determine that focusing only on interpreting the teammates' comments easily leads students to the idea expressed in option B: The teammates are trying to encourage Jake because they are not confident that he will make the catch. Students can also argue for dismissing the other options because of a lack of evidence.

✓ *Pretend to be the author.*

Students can sometimes arrive at the correct answer to conclusion/inference items simply by putting themselves in the author's shoes. Students can try to envision what the author might have written in the passage in order to cause the readers to draw the conclusions that are presented as options. In this item, for instance, students could think about what the author would have had the teammates say in order to lead readers to think that Jake is an important member of the team

FIGURE 7.6　**Building a Case**

What does paragraph 2 say about . . .	Evidence
A . . . the teammates' thinking Jake is an important member of the team?	*Nothing. The teammates' remarks are not about Jake's importance on the team.*
B . . . the teammates not feeling confident that Jake will make the catch?	*It says two different teammates are giving him directions. The author uses the words* shouts, hollers, *and* commands *to tell Jake what to do. The teammates would not need to do these things if they were confident that Jake could catch the ball on his own.*
C . . . the teammates' confusion about why Jake isn't wearing his glove?	*Nothing. Paragraphs 1, 6, and 12 contain a mention of a glove, but not paragraph 2.*
D . . . teammates' knowledge that the sun is distracting to Jake?	*Nothing. The author mentions the "blinding rays," not the teammates.*

(option A) or to show that the teammates think Jake will not make the catch (option B). Figure 7.7 shows some of the words that the author might have had the teammates say.

Notice that in option B, the students might come very close or might actually use the same words that the author does to help lead readers to conclude the notion presented as an option. By pretending to be the author, one option sometimes stands out as viable while the others show themselves as clearly wrong.

FIGURE 7.7　**Pretending to Be the Author**

Option	What An Author Might Write
A　They think of Jake as an important member of the team.	"We're glad you're on our team, Jake!"
B　They are not confident that Jake will make the catch.	"You can do this, Jake!" "Don't be scared of the ball, Jake!"
C　They don't understand why Jake isn't wearing his glove.	"Where is your glove, Jake?" "Put on your glove, Jake!"
D　They know the blinding sun is distracting to Jake.	"Use your hand to block the sun, Jake."

Comparison/Contrast

What is similar about Jake's experiences playing football and baseball?

A His teammates cannot hear his calls.
B He plays in order to try to impress his peers.
C He does not feel visible to his teammates.
D He is not given the opportunity to prove himself.

Correct answer: C

Strategies

✓ *Recognize the item type.*

The word *similar* indicates that this item requires students to compare two things or experiences to determine what they have in common. Other key words in stems of comparison/contrast items include *same*, *alike*, *common*, *different*, and *difference*.

✓ *Think about the comparison in graphic form.*

In comparison/contrast items, a simple graphic organizer can help students think about the options. For instance, for a comparison/contrast item that asks about a similarity, students might consider using a Venn diagram, in which the correct answer to the item is the statement that would belong in the interlocking area of the circle, as shown in Figure 7.8.

Another option is a basic T-chart in which the correct answer to the item can be placed in both columns. Students can begin to think about which statement is correct for both situations by first putting all the options in the T-chart and crossing out those that can be safely eliminated. For instance, students might notice immediately that option D can be eliminated because Jake is given the opportunity to catch the ball and make a touchdown on the football field; unfortunately he fumbles and feels embarrassed as a result (see

FIGURE 7.8 **Venn Diagram**

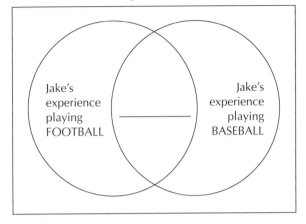

FIGURE 7.9 **Beginning of T-Chart Comparing Jake's Experiences**

Jake's experience playing FOOTBALL	Jake's experience playing BASEBALL
His teammates cannot hear his calls.	His teammates cannot hear his calls.
He plays in order to try to impress his peers.	He plays in order to try to impress his peers.
He does not feel visible to his teammates.	He does not feel visible to his teammates.
~~He is not given the opportunity to prove himself.~~	He is not given the opportunity to prove himself.

Figure 7.9). Therefore, because the statement is untrue about Jake's experience playing football, option D cannot be the correct answer. The T-chart, then, helps students realize that if the statement is untrue for either of the sports settings, football or baseball, then the option is not the correct answer.

✓ *Find paragraph references for the two things being compared.*

In this comparison/contrast item, the stem provides the two things that need to be compared: Jake's experiences playing football and Jake's experiences playing baseball. Students should return to the passage to find the paragraph references that relate to these two things as a whole. For example, students might note that paragraphs 3–5 are about Jake's playing football, and paragraphs 1–2 and 6–12 are about Jake's playing baseball. Then they can search within these paragraphs to determine if the ideas presented as the answer choices appear there.

Students who made a T-chart using the answer choices can make note of the paragraphs in which the answer choices are stated or implied, as shown in Figure 7.10.

Finding paragraph references to support the options helps students to realize that only option C presents an idea that is true of Jake's experiences in both football and baseball. The other options present ideas that are either untrue in both settings or are true of only one setting.

Searching for textual evidence to support the answer options also slows down students' thinking and requires that they carefully consider each option. For instance, students might recall references to teammates shouting on the sports fields, so option A might initially tempt them. That is, Jake's teammates call out to him to catch the ball in the first paragraph, and later in paragraphs 3 and 4, Jake calls out to the quarterback to gain his attention. However, if students return to the passage to take a closer look, they should realize that the idea in option A overstates what actually happens.

FIGURE 7.10 **T-Chart with Paragraph References Added**

Jake's experience playing FOOTBALL	Jake's experience playing BASEBALL
His teammates cannot hear his calls. (not there)	His teammates cannot hear his calls. (not there)
He plays in order to try to impress his peers. (not there)	He plays in order to try to impress his peers. (paragraph 12)
He does not feel visible to his teammates. (paragraphs 3 and 4)	He does not feel visible to his teammates. (paragraph 1)
He is not given the opportunity to prove himself. (not there)	He is not given the opportunity to prove himself. (not there)

Fact/Opinion

Which excerpt from the passage reveals the author's opinion?

A *. . . the too-tall, chubby, clumsy kid who, while respected on campus for guitar playing, is lost on the sports field.*

B *. . . I stick out my hands, grasp the ball, and pull it to my chest.*

C *I have fewer than five yards to go . . .*

D *I look down at the mound in the metal ball basket.*

Correct answer: A

Strategies

✓ *Recognize the item type.*

The word *opinion* clearly indicates that this item tests students' ability to distinguish an opinion from facts. An item asking students to identify a fact typically uses the word *fact* in the stem.

✓ *Have anchor examples.*

Students should be explicitly taught that when they see the words *fact* or *opinion* in an item stem, they are being asked to distinguish fact from opinion or opinion from fact. Therefore, in this item that assesses opinion, students should know that there will be only one opinion and that the other answer choices will contain facts.

To begin thinking about the distinction, students should recall a simple example of fact and opinion. For instance, a student might use anchor examples similar to these:

> *I was born on December 25, 1994. (fact)*
> *Cleaning my room is a waste of time. (opinion)*

From these examples, students can recognize that the first statement, a fact, can be verified, while the second statement is *their* opinion (but not likely the viewpoint of their *parents*). Students can then use what they glean about facts and opinions from the anchor examples to evaluate the options.

✓ *Look for signal words.*

Sometimes statements of opinion can be detected because of signal words and/or judgment words. Some signal words include *think, believe, suppose, feel, probably, perhaps, usually, sometimes,* and *often.* Some judgment words include *good, bad, great, best, worst,* and other such adjectives.

In this item, option A has a string of judgment words, such as *too-tall, chubby,* and *clumsy.*

✓ *Locate the statement in the passage to understand the context.*

In fact/opinion items, the four answer choices are statements from the passage that are plucked from their context. Many times, not having a good understanding of the context in which the statement is made adds to the difficulty of the item. Encourage students to find each option in the passage and mark the paragraph reference. Then simply reading the sentences that come before and after each answer choice can reacquaint students with the context and help reveal the statement as either a fact or an opinion.

✓ *Reread each paragraph but leave out the statement.*

Sometimes it is easier to figure out whether a statement is fact or opinion by thinking about what information would be missing if the author had left out the statement.

Students can reread the paragraph, skip over the statement that serves as the answer choice, and ask themselves, "Is a fact or opinion needed there?"

For instance, in option B, it is important for readers to know that Jake reaches for the ball and catches it; without this *fact,* the rest of the action of that paragraph would not make sense.

In option A, on the other hand, it is important for readers to know Jake's view of himself and how he thinks his peers view him; otherwise, readers would not know why it is such a big deal that a baseball is heading toward Jake. This *opinion* tells readers a great deal about his role or status on the team.

✓ *Construct try-out sentences to detect the opinion statement.*

Simply adding a version of "It is someone's opinion that . . ." to each option can help students determine which statement best reflects an opinion:

A   *It is someone's opinion that* Jake is chubby and clumsy and lost on the sports field.

B   *It is someone's opinion that* Jake sticks out his hands and pulls the football to his chest.

C   *It is someone's opinion that* Jake has fewer than five yards to run with the football.

D   *It is someone's opinion that* Jake looks at the balls in the metal basket.

Trying out the options in this way helps students detect which statement is really an opinion and that the others are facts. Students should respond to the statement made in option A by saying, "Yes, it's the author's/narrator's opinion of himself—and probably the opinion of his peers as well." Students should respond to option B by saying, "No, it is not an opinion that Jake catches the ball. He actually does; it is verifiable by those around him. B is a fact." For option C, students should recognize that the distance that Jake has to run can be measured, so it's a verifiable fact. Option D also contains a fact—Jake really does look at the balls in the metal basket.

Prediction

Which prediction about the narrator can be supported?

A   Jake will try harder in gym class.
B   Jake will be asked by his peers to play more often.
C   Jake will receive an award from the coach.
D   Jake will give up playing guitar for baseball.

Correct answer: A

Strategies

✓ *Recognize the item type.*

The word *prediction* in the item stem indicates that this item assesses understanding of prediction.

Alternate versions of prediction items are presented in Figure 7.11.

✓ *Summarize how the passage ends.*

Because a prediction item usually asks about what will happen in the future, the best starting place to ponder this item is at the end of the passage. It makes little sense to think about the beginning of the passage because the narrator/main character can change in significant ways. In this passage, Jake usually loathes gym class, but because he has an experience that changes his perspective significantly by the end, it makes sense that readers would make predictions about Jake based on the latest information they know about him.

Rereading a significant chunk of the text's ending helps ground students; they will know what the narrator/main character is saying and doing when the story ends. So, before trying to determine a logical next step in the action, students should first summarize the last moments of the story. They might do so as follows:

> *After successfully catching a ball and receiving praise from peers, Jake goes to gym class the next day but is nevertheless chosen last. Undaunted, Jake takes his place in right field and is hopeful about doing well again.*

Once a summary is formulated, students can begin thinking through each answer choice.

✓ *Don't be drawn to options that are appealing but unsupported.*

Prediction items tend to have options that are phrased in positive, pleasant ways. For instance, option B, "Jake will be asked by his peers to play more often," is certainly a situation that students will find appealing; after all, what middle school student isn't pleased by the acknowledgment of his or her peers? And option C, "Jake will receive an award from the coach," is a nice thing as well.

The problem with these options is that there is little evidence to support that either will happen, given the direction of the plot. Perhaps these events *could* happen, but students shouldn't argue themselves into believing that these events *will* happen.

Wrong options in prediction items are those that readers *cannot know* as a result of what is told in the plot or what is revealed about the typical behaviors of the characters. For example, while Jake has a better attitude about playing ball, readers cannot know whether his peers consider him

FIGURE 7.11 **Alternate Versions of Prediction Items**

If the story had continued, what would *most likely have happened?*

In the future, Jake will likely—

What do you think will happen *the next time* Jake _____?

What *will probably happen* after _____?

FIGURE 7.12   **Building a Case**

Option	Evidence
A Jake will try harder in gym class.	*Yes.* *Jake says that he has a desire to improve his ranking.* *Jake puts on his glove instead of leaving it on the ground, which means that he hopes to be able to use it.* *Jake's glove covers up his watch, which means that he will not be staring at it in hopes that gym class will be over soon.* *Jake hustles to right field, whereas before he just languished there "like a prisoner."* *Jake says he will no longer be bothered by the Texas sun or let it keep him from paying attention in case a ball comes his way again.*
D Jake will give up playing guitar for baseball.	*No.* *Paragraphs 2 and 12 mention that Jake is respected for his guitar playing, but these references don't suggest that he will choose something he is not very good at over something he is.*

any better a player because he caught one ball; in fact, being picked last again runs counter to this idea. Option B is something readers cannot know.

Option C suggests that the coach is so impressed by Jake's having caught one ball that he gives Jake an award. But readers cannot know whether the coach has any intention of handing out an award, because there is no mention of his doing so. Therefore, option C is something readers cannot know.

✓ *Build a case.*

Even though prediction items ask students to project an event beyond the text, they should still be able to find textual evidence to support the prediction; that's why building a case is a good strategy. See Figure 7.12 for "the case" for options A and D.

Trying to build a case for an option that is wrong (option D, for example) usually helps students to see that much less evidence exists than they might have thought. Finding a great deal of evidence to support option A—almost overwhelmingly so—indicates that it is the clear correct answer.

Supporting Evidence

Which sentence best shows a change in the narrator's attitude?

A *Every day is the same in my eighth-grade gym class.*

B *I figure one fewer ball in the equipment locker won't matter.*

C *The truth is that the next day, when teams were being picked, I stood there, the best guitar player around, and was chosen—last.*

D *Not even the intense Texas sun could keep me from watching the sky for a ball heading my way.*

Correct answer: D

Strategies

✓ *Recognize the item type.*

The words *which sentence best shows* and the italicized sentences in the options indicate to students that they must support an idea presented in the item stem with specific evidence from the passage. The words *shows a change in the narrator's attitude* present the idea that is supported by one of the four sentences that compose the options.

✓ *Contextualize each option.*

Many times, not having a good understanding of the context in which the sentence is made adds to the difficulty of a supporting evidence item. Simply reading the statements that come before and after each answer choice can reacquaint students with the context and help reveal whether the sentence connects with the idea in the item stem or not. (Once students find the sentences in the passage, they might want to write the paragraph number next to each option in case they need to reread the sentence later.)

Sometimes there are clues *within* the lifted sentences themselves. In this item, the key words are *change in attitude*, and students know that an attitude can be either positive or negative. In option D, the words *Not even the intense Texas sun could keep me from* show determination, or a positive attitude, and readers readily understand that Jake's attitude is fairly negative throughout the passage; therefore, the sentence in this option seems to signal a change. By contrast, in option A, the words *Every day is the same* seem to signal the opposite of change, so this option is not likely correct.

✓ *Answer the question yourself.*

A supporting evidence item asks students to support a conclusion or assertion that is provided; in this case the assertion is that Jake has a change in attitude. However, the item stem does not indicate whether the change was from a positive to a negative attitude or vice versa. So, students should first ask themselves, "What is Jake's change in attitude?" and then use the answer to this question to think through the meaning of the sentence in each option.

Students who think about the conflict and resolution and/or the organization of the passage can determine that Jake is initially miserable in gym class (negative attitude) but an experience causes him to want to do better (positive attitude). Then with this lens, students can read each option to see which signals the negative-to-positive change in Jake's attitude. Option D is the only one that shows that Jake has a fresh take on his situation.

Chapter 8

Text Matters

This chapter presents information about the most common types of items used to assess text matters on reading assessments. These include author's purpose and author's organization. The following are examples, not particular to any state, of reading standards for text matters. Students are expected to do the following:

- Identify an *author's purpose* for writing
- Recognize common patterns of *organization* (such as cause-effect, chronological, and problem-solution) used by an author to express ideas

Basic Strategies for Text Matters Items

The following basic strategies are good starting points for teachers to share with students as they work together to make sense of reading test items about text matters. Later in this chapter, strategies that are specific to certain types of text matters items are explored.

✓ *Recognize the item type.*

Author's purpose. Items assessing students' ability to identify an author's purpose for writing usually include the word *purpose* or the words *author's purpose* in the item stem. Essentially, authors write to entertain, inform, or persuade. But these *three* purposes present a problem for test makers who write multiple-choice items with *four* options. So, in middle school assessments, students are expected to navigate these "variations" on purposes: define, describe, explain, inform, illustrate, demonstrate, compare, list, entertain, tell, relate, persuade, and convince. Purpose items can ask about the entire passage, multiple paragraphs or a section of text, or a single paragraph of the passage.

Author's organization. Items assessing students' ability to recognize an organizational pattern usually include the word *organize* or *organization*. Organization items can cover the entire passage, or items can ask about a portion of the passage, especially when authors change the pattern for a specific reason.

✓ *Have anchor examples.*

Author's purpose (and text type). Students should learn to associate certain purposes with text types. As examples, fact-based newspaper articles (text type) should be associated with the purpose "inform"; advertisements and editorials (text type) should be associated with the purpose "persuade"; instructional manuals (text type) should be associated with the purpose "explain" or "list steps." Anchor examples that prepare students to recognize an author's purpose should be built around discussions about text types.

Author's organization. Some organizational patterns can be difficult to detect because they cannot be exclusively linked to certain text types (as is often the case with an author's purposes for writing). For instance, an informational passage might use a problem-solution or cause-effect structure, but a narrative passage could as well. Furthermore, students have to make sure to think about the pattern the author uses, rather than the content of the ideas. For example, an author might talk about the cause of a problem within a text, but the structure might be chronological. As a result, students need many opportunities to analyze how an author organizes ideas within a text. Anchor examples for the most common organizational patterns can help students recognize these same structures in the passages they encounter on assessments.

Author's Purpose

The purpose of this passage is to—

A   compare playing baseball to playing football

B   encourage readers to participate in sports

C   explain the value of playing baseball and football

D   tell about one boy's experiences playing sports

Correct answer: D

Strategies

✓ *Recognize the item type.*

The word *purpose* indicates that this item tests an author's purpose for writing.

Alternate versions of purpose items are presented in Figure 8.1.

✓ *Match text type and purpose words.*

Students should be taught that purposes for writing are often tied to text types. As examples, persuasive writing (purpose) might take the form of a flyer or newspaper editorial (text types), and a fact-filled magazine article (text type) is meant to inform (purpose).

FIGURE 8.1 **Alternate Versions of Purpose Items**

Purpose items can ask about a particular paragraph, a group of paragraphs, a particular feature of a text, or a passage as a whole, as shown in the examples below.

What is the purpose of paragraph X?

Why does the author include paragraphs X and Y?

What is the most likely reason that the author provides the photograph?

The author wrote this passage probably to tell readers—

Students who can identify the text type as reflective or personal writing should be able to determine that the words *tell* and *experiences* in option D best match the purpose of this passage.

✓ *Have anchor examples.*

Because some purposes are more difficult for students to detect than others, discussions about an author's purpose are best tied to text types and features (as noted in the previous strategy), and multiple examples of genres help students recognize both purposes and text types more easily.

In this case, students who have read widely in the genres of autobiography, memoir, and personal essay will readily notice the use of the first person point of view and that the text is composed of personal experiences. Students should connect that the author is sharing an experience—particularly how a past experience (in fourth grade) comes to bear on a later one (in eighth grade). Option D best describes the purpose.

Two activities about author's purpose on pages 184 and 185 can help familiarize students with purpose words commonly used on an assessment as well as offer anchor examples.

✓ *Ask a key question.*

Students can think through the answer choices by posing a question about the key word in each option, with knowledge of simple definitions/features of those purposes:

A   Is this passage meant to provide information by comparing two things—baseball and football?

B   Is this passage meant to motivate readers to take action of some kind—playing sports?

C   Is this passage meant to inform readers about the value of two sports?

D   Is this passage meant to convey to readers how the narrator feels about something—playing sports?

By answering these questions, some purposes will be particularly easy to eliminate. For instance, option B, to "encourage readers to participate in sports," seems contrary to the narrator's feelings of ineptitude on a sports field; students will realize that the passage is not a celebration of participation in sports! That same thinking can be applied to dismiss option C, to "explain the value of playing baseball and football."

Asking and answering these key questions also invites students to avoid considering simply the content of the passages, but to think critically about the author's decision to write the passage as he or she has done. For instance, in option A, but events involving both baseball and football are part of the passage, these episodes provide readers with insight about the narrator; they do not inform readers about the sports themselves. So, when students construct the key question "Is this passage meant to provide information by comparing two things?" they should recognize that the author is not trying to make the reader more informed about sports.

That leaves option D as a clear standout. Students should recognize that the passage, from start to finish, is bent on relating Jake's often unfortunate experiences on the sports field. Literary nonfiction is about the author; sports are merely the vehicle for allowing us to learn about the author. Option D is correct.

✓ *Picture the texts.*

Students should try to picture the kinds of texts that would match the purposes that are presented as answer choices. For instance, in option A, students should wonder if a text with a purpose of comparing playing baseball to playing football would "look" and "sound" like this passage. Students should recognize that a text with the purpose of comparing two sports would have to *inform* readers about a few aspects of those sports—such as which one requires more skill, or has more rules, or needs more players. Such an expository text might include drawings, photographs, sidebars listing rules, and so forth.

For options B and C, students might picture a flyer or poster that provides reasons for students to consider participating in sports. The language of the flyer or poster would likely be encouraging or motivating.

For option D, students should determine that telling about one's experiences takes a story form, and this passage certainly looks and sounds like a story. Option D, then, is correct.

Author's Organization

The author develops this passage by—

A comparing and contrasting two sports
B switching back and forth in time
C relating the events in the order in which they occur
D relating information from most to least important

Correct answer: B

Strategies

✓ *Recognize the item type.*

The word *develops* tells students that this item tests author's organization.

Alternate versions of author's organization items are presented in Figure 8.2.

✓ *Have anchor examples.*

Students need anchor examples that can help them determine the organization of a reading passage on an assessment. If students have an anchor example of flashback, they should be able to recognize that in this passage, the author switches between two important settings (playing baseball in the fourth grade and playing football in the eighth grade). Furthermore, students' anchor examples of the organizational patterns that compose the three distractors in this item should help students eliminate them as viable.

The activity on page 186 can help to provide students with anchor features and examples.

✓ *Ask a key question.*

The answer choices for author's organization items contain key words that can be formulated into basic questions:

A Are two sports being compared?
  What information tells how the sports are alike and different?

FIGURE 8.2 Alternate Versions of Author's Organization Items

Items assessing the organization of a passage ask about sections of the text or about the text as a whole. The following list presents some of the answer choices that are used to answer the question *How is the passage organized?*

in order of importance

from most important to least important

in the order in which events happen

by placing events in the order they happened

by presenting a cause and then its effects

by comparing two or more things

by describing several places

by presenting questions and answers

by giving step-by-step instructions

by presenting two sides of an issue

by presenting main ideas and supporting evidence

B Do some events take place in a different time than others?
C Are the events told according to when they happened?
D Does the most important information appear first? Does the least important information appear last?

Certainly, the best way for students to approach answering these key questions is to use their knowledge of text types. For instance, students will have no trouble determining that this passage is storylike, and only options B and C present organizational patterns that are appropriate for stories. Options A and D are easily dismissed, because students know that these patterns are more appropriate for nonfiction (especially option A) and nonfiction and/or persuasive writing (especially option D).

✓ *Find paragraph references using the "chunk and jot down" strategy.*

Encourage students to make paragraph references for the patterns used as options in an author's organization item:

A   Comparison and contrast (nowhere)

B   Switching back and forth in time (eighth grade, paragraphs 1–2; fourth grade, paragraphs 3–5; eighth grade, paragraphs 6–12)

C   Chronology (paragraphs 1–2, but not after that)

D   Most to least important (nowhere)

Using the "chunk and jot down" strategy (explained in Chapter 4), students can divide the passage into manageable chunks and more clearly see the organization of the passage. By determining that one setting is established in paragraphs 1 and 2 and that the setting shifts at the beginning of paragraph 3 and then again in paragraph 6, students will recognize that the author is purposefully shifting time. So, option B is the clear correct answer.

Putting Strategies to Work

Strategies are meant to be used; otherwise they are of no use. This section is designed with that principle in mind—that students need useful strategies and high-quality test preparation materials to read, ponder, and explore so ultimately they can demonstrate their strategic thinking about reading and tests.

The materials in this section provide a variety of passages, short and long, that are similar to those that students will encounter on most reading assessments. The passages include those in the genres of realistic fiction, poetry, practical/procedural reading, expository writing, and persuasive writing. Also common on middle school assessments are paired passages, so the persuasive passage ("Bad Sports") is intended to be paired with the passage "The Gym Class ~~Nobody~~ Somebody" (presented in the previous section).

Following each passage is a variety of items from the categories explored in Section 2, which are the most commonly assessed standards on reading tests. Next to each item are tips for thinking through the item. Because teacher modeling of strategies for reading and test taking is valuable for students (Fuhrken and Roser 2010; Johnson 1998), the tips can be used by teachers to help guide students toward understanding and applying the strategies explained in Section 2. Teachers may also use the tips to construct mini-lessons for each sample item or for a particular strategy that is new to students. The goal of Section 3 is to provide an array of test preparation materials that teachers can tailor to their students' needs.

In addition, this section ends with a reprint of the passage and sample items that compose Section 2. Teachers may want this material in a compact form so that they can use it as the basis of think-alouds, for mini-lessons, or for other discussions with students as they build understandings of strategies that work.

Answers and explanations appear at the end of this section.

Reaching for Fame

1   Jamal walked up to the picnic table and plunked down a huge book, startling Rebecca.

2   "What's with the book?" she asked.

3   "That resource, my friend, is my guide to fame," he announced.

4   *Another one of Jamal's wild ideas*, Rebecca thought to herself, but she was intrigued enough to <u>engage</u> him further. She eyed the front cover, which read *Guinness World Records.*

5   "I know all about that," she said. "The other night on TV, a man set a record by using a rope to pull an airplane weighing over a hundred tons. I bet you can't do that!"

6   "I *know* I can't do that. But I *am* going to do something to get my name in this book," Jamal countered.

7   The banter ended there since it was time to return to class. Rebecca soon forgot all about the record book. But Jamal didn't. Over the next few days, he studied the rules and researched other people's records. Although eager to be famous, he hadn't found a record he thought he could set or break.

8   Then that afternoon, right before his eyes, he found his answer. Or so he thought. Jamal's mother had made thirty cupcakes before she realized that his sister's class didn't need them until the next week.

9   Jamal grabbed the record book. "Cupcakes . . . cupcakes," he murmured as he flipped the pages. *Perfect*, he thought, *there's no record yet for the most cupcakes eaten.*

10   "I'll get rid of these for you, Mom," he told his mother, and with that, he was off to Rebecca's house.

11   When Rebecca came to the front porch, she saw the cupcakes and the record book. She knew instantly what her friend wanted to do.

12   "I need a witness," he said. "I'm going to eat thirty cupcakes in thirty seconds."

13   "Are you sure?" Rebecca asked, with a bit of concern in her voice. "That's one per second. You'll have to swallow them whole."

14   Jamal grabbed his first cupcake confidently. Because Rebecca could tell that he could not be <u>deterred</u>, she said, "All right then. Get ready." When the second hand on her watch reached twelve, she shouted, "Go."

15   Jamal shoved the cupcake into his mouth. He gulped it down without much trouble and reached for the second one. Rebecca watched, amazed. Frosting smeared his face. Chocolate sprinkles leaped from the cupcakes and landed on the porch. But Jamal's feverish pace then slowed considerably. A few seconds later, Rebecca yelled, "Stop."

16   Jamal and Rebecca counted three empty cupcake wrappers.

17   "That's all?" Jamal questioned. "That's definitely not record-setting! And I feel as though I ate 200!"

18   His hopes dashed, Jamal realized that eating cupcakes was not so easy.

19   Rebecca was a little <u>disheartened</u> too. "Don't frown, my friend," she said. "Besides, do you really want to become famous for being really, really hungry one afternoon?"

20   She browsed the book's page and offered new ideas. "Maybe you should try building a house with matchsticks!" As Rebecca looked up, they both dissolved into laughter.

21   Shortly afterward, Jamal said goodbye. He wanted to go home and continue searching for the perfect idea. But first he needed to lie in bed until he felt better.

Answers and their explanations for the items about "Reaching for Fame" begin on page 124.

1. In paragraph 14, the word <u>deterred</u> means—

   A criticized
   B determined
   C prepared
   D discouraged

   • Look for clues in paragraph 14. What does "All right then" tell about Rebecca's thoughts?
   • Since all answer choices are verbs, substitute each answer choice for the tested word in the passage.
   • Think about the tone of paragraphs 13 and 14. Jamal shows confidence, whereas Rebecca is concerned. How do these clues help?

2. Which words from paragraphs 16–20 help readers know the meaning of <u>disheartened</u> in paragraph 19?

   A *counted, questioned*
   B *hopes dashed, frown*
   C *realized, want to become famous*
   D *offered, dissolved into laughter*

   • The tested word appears in this sentence: "Rebecca was a little disheartened too." The word *too* indicates that Rebecca feels the same as Jamal, disappointed.
   • Look for words in paragraphs 16–20 that express what it means to be disappointed.

3. Read the dictionary entry below.

   engage [en-geyj'] v. 1. to bind, as by pledge, promise, or contract 2. to occupy the attention or efforts of another 3. to secure for employment or use 4. to enter into conflict with another

   Which definition best matches how the word <u>engage</u> is used in paragraph 4?

   A Definition 1
   B Definition 2
   C Definition 3
   D Definition 4

   • Reread paragraph 4 and come up with another word for *engage.*
   • Look for key words in the definitions and try substituting them into the tested sentence.

4. What event most helps Jamal decide on an idea to pursue?

   A He studies the record book.
   B He talks to Rebecca about the man she saw set a record.
   C He learns that his mother does not need the cupcakes she baked.
   D He reads about the rules.

   • The question identifies a plot event. Find it in the passage and reread to get the context.

5. Rebecca is presented throughout the passage mostly as—

   A   jealous
   B   stubborn
   C   talented
   D   caring

- Another way to think about the question is: *In this story, Rebecca acts mostly _____.*
- Remember to think about Rebecca's actions *throughout* the passage. Find several plot events to support your answer.

---

6. Which of these contributes most to the conflict of the passage?

   A   Jamal finds it harder to achieve fame than he anticipates.
   B   Rebecca thinks Jamal has unrealistic expectations.
   C   Jamal's classes take up time he could use to study the record book.
   D   Jamal needs someone to witness his record-setting attempt.

- Is the conflict internal (in a character's mind) or external (shown through the events of a character)?
- If external, ask yourself what the main character wants and what stands in the way.

---

7. Which sentence is an example of personification?

   A   *Jamal walked up to the picnic table and plunked down a huge book, startling Rebecca.*
   B   *"That resource, my friend, is my guide to fame," he announced.*
   C   *"Are you sure?" Rebecca asked, with a bit of concern in her voice.*
   D   *Chocolate sprinkles leaped from the cupcakes and landed on the porch.*

- Recall a definition or example of personification.
- Find something nonhuman doing something human.

---

8. Read these sentences from paragraph 8.

   Then that afternoon, right before his eyes, he found his answer. Or so he thought.

   These sentences are an example of—

   A   personification
   B   metaphor
   C   foreshadowing
   D   symbolism

- Think about what you know about the techniques listed in the answer choices.
- Do the sentences give human qualities to something nonhuman (A), make a direct comparison (B), hint at a future event (C), or represent an abstract concept (D)?

9. What happens right after Jamal eats the cupcakes?

    A   Jamal figures that he has not set a record.

    B   Rebecca tries to make Jamal feel better.

    C   Jamal goes home because he does not feel well.

    D   Rebecca offers Jamal another idea for setting a record.

- The question identifies a plot event. Find it in the passage and reread to get the context.
- Find the answer choices in the passage and determine which comes next in time order.

No Matter Where We've Been

By Walt McDonald

I swore I'd never come home
to the Plains, eight hundred acres
and stars so bright they buzzed.

I said I'd work these rows only for sport,
5   maize for a pair of calves.
Goats and hawks are hobbies, a pond

with bass once in a hundred casts.
Old Uncle Bubba told me
no matter where I've been,

10   it's home. Our boys make a fortune
dragging home rattlers in towsacks.
The prairie crawls with tarantulas,

hawks in all weather, gliding on thermals
There's little we could lose, here,
15   little we could hide. We've almost

stopped pretending clouds are mountains,
here where rain is rare as trees.
If we can't accept these fields,

our souls with all their wind
20   and cactus, we ought to leave.
Even at night, our shadows sprawl:

that moon is up for hours. On fields
this flat, someone's easy to find
and always calls us friend.

Answers and their explanations for the items about "No Matter Where We've Been" begin on page 125.

1. In line 12, the poet's use of the word <u>crawls</u> suggests that tarantulas are—

   A cherished
   B dangerous
   C mysterious
   D abundant

   - Reread the descriptions surrounding line 12 for possible clues.
   - In place of *crawls*, try adding in the answer choices to line 12: The prairie is _____ with tarantulas.

2. Which words from the poem are an example of hyperbole?

   A *stars so bright they buzzed*
   B *dragging home rattlers in towsacks*
   C *We've almost stopped pretending clouds are mountains*
   D *On fields this flat*

   - Recall a definition or example of hyperbole.
   - Find an exaggerated idea.

3. Which of these statements best captures the poem's theme?

   A Living life on the Plains is unique and special.
   B Friendships can endure any hardships.
   C Nature is awe-inspiring and beautiful.
   D Rugged living teaches us who we are.

   - Focus on key words and think about whether they represent a big idea in the poem.
   - Try to find details in the poem that serve as evidence of the theme.

4. What can readers determine from the first three lines and the last three lines?

   A The speaker misses the Plains in the evenings.
   B The speaker left the Plains for a while but has returned.
   C The speaker feels that the people of the Plains are kind.
   D The speaker was raised in an area of the Plains that is large.

   - Reread both sets of lines and think about what they have in common.
   - Decide which answer choice presents an idea that is represented in both sets of lines.

5. How does the poet develop the main idea of the poem?

    A   By listing each of the animals that can be found on the Plains

    B   By explaining that living on the Plains requires a great deal of work

    C   By describing the qualities of the Plains that the speaker values

    D   By suggesting that the speaker has accepted the harshness of the Plains

- This question asks how the poet presents his thoughts/ideas.
- Think also about the purpose of the poem.
- Consider each answer choice by trying to find multiple pieces of text as support.

Sizzling Hot Summer Camps

The David Scott Youth Foundation is offering three new and exciting summer camps: videogame creation, acting, and martial arts training. (Visit our Web site for more options.) The summer camps are entirely FREE! It's the most fun you can have indoors.

Get Gaming **Camp** *(60 hours)*

If you could spend every waking moment involved in videogames (and if your parents would allow it), then "Get Gaming" Camp is right for you!

<u>What You Will Learn and Be Able to Do</u>
"Get Gaming" Camp is taught by award-winning videogame developers. The classes are designed to help beginners . . .

- create characters,
- craft a storyline, and
- select a soundtrack.

By the end of the camp, participants will not only be better game players, but they'll have authored their own game.

<u>Who Can Participate</u>
Open to middle school and high school students.
Not for the only-slightly-interested videogamer, this camp requires a five-day-a-week, two-month commitment, beginning June 9.

<u>What You Need</u>
All equipment and materials provided.

Star Status **Camp** *(24 hours)*

Go from backstage to front and center!

<u>What You Will Learn and Be Able to Do</u>
Actors will . . .

- act in scenes,
- try improvisational acting, and
- receive voice training.

On the last day, participants perform for families and friends in a talent showcase.

<u>Who Can Participate</u>
Novice and experienced actors ages 5–15 who can attend from June 18 to July 18.

<u>What You Need</u>
A desire to learn to take the stage!

Kung Fu for Youth **Camp** *(20 hours)*

Learn the traditions and power of Kung Fu in this intensive half-day camp.

<u>What You Will Learn and Be Able to Do</u>
Participants will . . .

- build fitness,
- increase focus, and
- improve technique.

<u>Who Can Participate</u>
Beginning and advanced martial artists, ages 9 and up, are welcome from July 11 to July 15.

<u>What You Need</u>
Come dressed in casual clothing.

For more details or to register, call (555) 701-2375. Space is limited, so sign up TODAY!

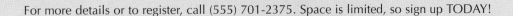

Answers and their explanations for the items about "Sizzling Hot Summer Camps" begin on page 126.

1. Friends and families can attend the last day of acting camp on—

    A   June 9
    B   July 11
    C   July 15
    D   July 18

- Focus on the acting camp and locate the mention of dates.

2. Readers can draw the conclusion that the three camps—

    A   were the most popular among campers last year
    B   provide most of the materials the campers will need to participate
    C   are the only ones being offered this summer
    D   are taught by students who have attended the camps in the past

- The word *conclusion* means the answer will not be stated in the passage.
- The words *three camps* indicate that something must be true for all three camps.
- Read each answer choice and try to find information that makes the answer choice wrong; then you can find information for the remaining answer choice that you think is right.

3. Which camp could be attended by students who want to commit only a week of their free time?

    A   "Get Gaming" Camp
    B   "Star Status" Camp
    C   "Kung Fu for Youth" Camp
    D   None of the camps

- Focus on the attendance dates of each camp to determine the answer.

4. Which of these is an opinion in the passage?

    A   *It's the most fun you can have indoors.*
    B   *"Get Gaming" Camp is taught by award-winning videogame developers.*
    C   *On the last day, participants perform for families and friends in a talent showcase.*
    D   *Come dressed in casual clothing.*

- Look for any descriptive or tone words that signal opinions.
- Add *It's someone's opinion that* to the beginning of each answer choice.

5. What is the purpose of the sections titled "What You Will Learn and Be Able to Do"?

    A   To explain to readers who will be teaching the camps

    B   To convince readers that the camps will be enjoyable

    C   To describe to readers what the campers will do on the last day

    D   To provide readers with an idea of what to expect at the camps

- Think about the type of information you would see in a section titled "What You Will Learn and Be Able to Do."
- Try to find at least two details in those sections that serve as evidence of the answer you choose.

6. The purpose of the passage is to—

    A   persuade readers to be more active

    B   inform readers about the camps that are available

    C   ask readers to support the foundation

    D   explain to readers how to plan their summer

- Think about the type of text the passage is.
- Picture in your mind what the text that each answer choice describes would look like.

Face Facts About Mount Rushmore

By Jerome Jones

Some facts about the carvings on Mount Rushmore are well known. Where is the monument located? South Dakota. Which four presidents' faces are featured? Washington, Jefferson, Roosevelt, and Lincoln.

But the story of Mount Rushmore is filled with many more intriguing facts. Let's dig in to four that you might not have known, until now.

1. Presidents weren't in the original plans.

In 1923, Doane Robinson wanted to create something so original in the Black Hills of South Dakota that people would flock to the locale. Fascinated by legends of the Wild West, Robinson wanted to look up to the faces of George Armstrong Custer, Buffalo Bill Cody, Lewis and Clark, and Sioux warriors.

But when sculptor Gutzon Borglum accepted Robinson's job offer in 1924, Borglum was not interested in memorializing regional heroes. He argued that the monument should be timeless in its relevance to history. Borglum, evidently, was a persuasive man, since Robinson agreed to a carving of George Washington. In 1925, when the project was funded, President Coolidge insisted that a Democrat and two Republicans be represented as well, hence the three other presidents that appear today.

2. The mountain cliff was Plan B.

Robinson's Plan A for the carvings was a region called the Needles, an area containing numerous individual towers, or pillars, of granite. When Borglum surveyed the site, though, he found it to be unacceptable. He believed the granite was brittle and the pillars were too thin to support the sculptures. Because Robinson had no Plan B, Borglum left.

Returning a year later, Borglum and his party went climbing, and Borglum was awe-struck when he took in the panorama of Mount Rushmore. Borglum inspected the mountain cliff and determined its granite was free from breaks and had good sun exposure. He had found his site.

3. Thomas Jefferson was a second "draft."

Borglum's initial survey of the mountain cliff clearly needed a closer look. Once the carving of Washington was complete, work began on carving Thomas Jefferson on Washington's *right* side. However, after eighteen months, workers found that the granite was too badly cracked to continue in that spot. Jefferson had to be dynamited off the mountain and begun again on the left side of Washington.

4. Visitors today often are treated to a cultural lesson.

Each year, several million visitors stare up at the inspiring carvings of the four presidents. A monument visit offers a lesson in cultures as well. On any given day, visitors might try Lakota hoop dancing, watch Norwegians dance, whittle wood with Germans, paint Sioux pottery, or hear a multicultural choir. Superintendent Gerard Baker, in the PBS program *Mount Rushmore: Telling America's Stories*, explains that the memorial today seeks to highlight the various cultures that make up America.

And You Might Not Have Known . . .
- A 39-by-70 foot flag, made by women of Rapid City, South Dakota, was used to cover each face prior to an unveiling ceremony.
- At the Thomas Jefferson unveiling ceremony, President Roosevelt, who was not scheduled to speak, spontaneously shared, "I had no conception, until about ten minutes ago, not only of its magnitude, but also its permanent beauty and importance."
- Susan B. Anthony would have been the fifth face on the mountain but for a lack of funding.
- No deaths from injuries or accidents occurred during the massive and dangerous construction.

Answers and their explanations for the items about "Face Facts About Mount Rushmore" begin on page 127.

1. Readers can use knowledge of the prefix *pan-* to determine that <u>panorama</u> means—

   A partial view
   B opposite view
   C wide view
   D wrong view

   - Think of the meaning of *pan-* or words that use the prefix *pan-*.
   - Substitute each answer choice for the tested word in the passage.

2. In the section titled "And You Might Not Have Known," the word <u>spontaneously</u> means—

   A with a critical tone
   B in a childlike manner
   C among friends
   D without being planned

   - Look for a clue within the bulleted information near where the tested word appears.
   - The sentence structure indicates that the word describes President Roosevelt's actions. What does the phrase following his name suggest?

3. What is the main idea of the section titled "Presidents weren't in the original plans"?

   A Borglum and President Coolidge revised Robinson's proposal for the project.
   B Robinson wanted to find a way to entice people to visit the Black Hills.
   C Borglum did not think that the Wild West was an important era to memorialize.
   D Robinson asked President Coolidge to help expand the proposal for the project.

   - What idea did you jot down next to this section when you read the passage?
   - Ask yourself, "What is the one thing the author really needs me to know about the information in this section?"
   - Select a big idea rather than a small detail.

4. As a construction site, the Needles was rejected because—

   A Robinson was not familiar with the area
   B the region was not approved for funding
   C Borglum was not available to survey it
   D the quality of the resources was thought to be poor

   - The word *because* tells you that the question and the answer form a cause-effect relationship. Another way of phrasing this is, "What caused the Needles to be rejected as a construction site?"
   - Reread the section of the passage that discusses the Needles.
   - For the answer you choose, find at least one sentence that states that answer (but in different words, probably).

5. Which of these sentences includes the author's opinion?

    A *Borglum's initial survey of the mountain cliff clearly needed a closer look.*

    B *Jefferson had to be dynamited off the mountain and begun again on the left side of Washington.*

    C *On any given day, visitors might try Lakota hoop dancing, watch Norwegians dance, whittle wood with Germans, paint Sioux pottery, or hear a multicultural choir.*

    D *Susan B. Anthony would have been the fifth face on the mountain but for a lack of funding.*

- Look for any descriptive or tone words that signal opinions.
- Add *It's the author's opinion that* to the beginning of each answer choice.

6. What is likely the author's reason for including the section titled "And You Might Not Have Known"?

    A To emphasize the idea that Mount Rushmore is relevant to our nation's history

    B To interest readers with more surprising facts about Mount Rushmore

    C To suggest that visitors to Mount Rushmore enjoy viewing Thomas Jefferson

    D To highlight that South Dakotans helped make Mount Rushmore possible

- Think about the type of information you would see in a section titled "And You Might Not Have Known."
- Focus on the purpose of the entire article and how that section contributes to that purpose.

Bad Sports

By Melissa Gaskill

1   I think we are taking youth sports way too seriously. Programs like Little League and Pop Warner Football were originally founded on the principles of letting every kid play and having fun, but many youth leagues now resemble miniature versions of professional sports. The frightening "do whatever it takes to win" mentality includes yelling at children, playing through pain, and even trying to injure other players. Winning has become more important than the kids having fun, more important than the kids themselves.

2   Maybe we need to be reminded that these are just kids. Our kids. I remember T-ball—my son and his teammates spent their time in the outfield pulling up dandelions or digging in the dirt. The grown-ups often hollered at these 5- and 6-year-olds to pay attention. Now I wonder why. We shouldn't have cared who won, just that the kids were outside and having fun.

3   I figured I was alone in my alarm until I read *Why Johnny Hates Sports* by Fred Engh. Engh says 70 percent of all youngsters drop out of organized sports by age 13 because of unpleasant experiences. Seventy percent. By age 13! Frankly, that seems to me about the age kids should start team sports, not already be burned out and quitting.

4   Sports, and team sports in particular, have a lot to teach children—when they're ready. Let's face it, 11-year-olds can get distracted or tired. So can 15-year-olds, but they usually have the developmental ability and maturity to push through it and give that extra effort. That feels like a real accomplishment, and teaches perseverance. But pushing an 11-year-old to act 15 won't make her develop or mature any faster. It might, however, make her drop out of sports.

5   Fortunately, my youngest has decided to move on to another sport rather than quit. My dandelion-picking son seems to have let all that yelling go in one ear and out the other (an annoying skill in so many arenas), going on from baseball to soccer, basketball, football and, finally, lacrosse. My oldest daughter has dabbled in a variety of sports as well (her favorite: Ultimate Frisbee, a game that defies rules and organization).

6   I'm glad about this. I'm not against sports or competition, just against taking them too seriously. Too much competition sucks the fun out. An undue emphasis on winning and losing—and not on teamwork, self-improvement, and good sportsmanship—takes away from the benefits sports can offer, like cooperation, respect for teammates and opponents, even compassion for the loser. I want my children—and their future coworkers, neighbors and spouses—to have exposure to those things, too.

7   Finally, I don't think we should sacrifice the fun of childhood. No one should know better than my success-oriented generation that you only get to be young once. I don't think my kids will look back from that vaunted front-porch rocking chair and say, "Gee, I wish I'd won more soccer games when I was 11." I know I won't.

Answers and their explanations for the items about "Bad Sports" begin on page 128.

1. Which of these best identifies the author's central argument?

    A   Playing to win rather than playing for fun has spoiled youth sports.

    B   Adults know better than to yell at kids at youth sports events.

    C   Pushing a child to grow up too fast is irresponsible.

    D   Some kids need to try multiple sports before finding an enjoyable one.

- A central argument or idea is supported throughout the passage. Look for the "big idea" that most paragraphs support.

---

2. What is likely the reason the author is not completely against team sports?

    A   She has not seen any player suffer a major injury.

    B   She thinks participating can teach kids important lessons.

    C   She knows that parents want to watch their kids play.

    D   She knows kids can drop out if they have a bad experience.

- The word *likely* indicates the answer is not stated in the passage; it must be inferred.
- The words *not completely against team sports* means the author must think playing sports has positive qualities. Look in the passage for what she says.
- Find at least two pieces of evidence to support your answer.

---

3. Which of these ideas found in the passage is best represented by the image?

    A   *letting every kid play*
    B   *do whatever it takes to win*
    C   *self-improvement*
    D   *respect for teammates*

- State in your own words what you think the image represents.
- Try to match your understanding of the image to one of the answer choices. Remember that images are chosen and placed purposefully to relate to a specific idea in the text.

4. Read this sentence from paragraph 6.

    An undue emphasis on winning and losing—and not on teamwork, self-improvement, and good sportsmanship— takes away from the benefits sports can offer, like cooperation, respect for teammates and opponents, even compassion for the loser.

    What is the author suggesting in this sentence?

    A   Being a member of a team is a skill best learned through playing sports.
    B   Some sports are geared more toward keeping score and declaring a winner than others.
    C   Young people have to be taught to take into account the feelings of their opponents.
    D   Pressure and competitiveness can take away from the positive aspects of playing sports.

- The word *suggesting* indicates that you have to infer the answer from the information provided.
- Try putting the excerpt in your own words and then matching it to one of the answer choices.

5. What is the most likely reason that the author includes information from Engh's book?

    A   To imply that kids today give up too quickly when trying new sports
    B   To suggest that parents are to blame for allowing kids to quit organized sports
    C   To emphasize that the majority of kids find organized sports unsatisfactory
    D   To establish that most kids do not develop the maturity that is needed to play sports

- The words *most likely reason* indicate that the answer must be inferred.
- Another way of asking this question is, "What point does the author make by mentioning Engh's book?"

The following questions ask about "Bad Sports" and "The Gym Class ~~Nobody~~ Somebody." Answers and their explanations for the items begin on page 128.

1. How does the tone of the passages differ?

   A The tone of "Bad Sports" is urgent, whereas the tone of "The Gym Class ~~Nobody~~ Somebody" is angry.

   B The tone of "Bad Sports" is dramatic, whereas the tone of "The Gym Class ~~Nobody~~ Somebody" is regretful.

   C The tone of "Bad Sports" is sympathetic, whereas the tone of "The Gym Class ~~Nobody~~ Somebody" is candid.

   D The tone of "Bad Sports" is critical, whereas the tone of "The Gym Class ~~Nobody~~ Somebody" is reflective.

   • Recall that tone refers to the author's attitude about (and approach to writing about) the topic.
   • Try picturing the authors talking about their subjects. How would they express themselves?
   • For the answer you choose, find at least two sentences that reflect the tone of each passage.

2. Which of these ideas is explored in "Bad Sports" and "The Gym Class ~~Nobody~~ Somebody"?

   A Playing sports is more important than academics in some schools.

   B Young people try to impress their peers when on the sports field.

   C Playing sports should be an enjoyable activity for young people.

   D Young people develop aggression as a result of playing sports.

   • For each answer choice, focus on one or two key words. For instance, answer choice A mentions academics. Which passage discusses the importance of academics— neither, one, or both?
   • After you choose your answer, find at least one piece of evidence from both passages.

3. What is a similarity between the authors of the passages?

   A The authors wrote from lived experiences.

   B The authors want to warn readers about the problems with sports.

   C The authors admit to being unsuccessful at sports when younger.

   D The authors want their children to find sports that suit them.

   • Think about a commonality between the authors that is provable.
   • For the answer you choose, be able to point to at least one piece of evidence from each passage.

4. The author of "The Gym Class ~~Nobody~~ Somebody" would most likely relate to which of these excerpts from "Bad Sports"?

   A   *. . . many youth leagues now resemble miniature versions of professional sports.*

   B   *. . . my son and his teammates spent their time in the outfield pulling up dandelions or digging in the dirt.*

   C   *Let's face it, 11-year-olds can get distracted or tired.*

   D   *We shouldn't have cared who won, just that the kids were outside and having fun.*

- Narrow in on the answer by thinking about details from "The Gym Class ~~Nobody~~ Somebody" that relate to the information in "Bad Sports."

Answers and Explanations

<table>
<tr><td colspan="3" align="center">"Reaching for Fame"</td></tr>
<tr><td align="center">Answer</td><td align="center">Skill</td><td align="center">Explanation</td></tr>
<tr><td>1. D</td><td>Context Clues</td><td>In the context of paragraph 14, the word deterred means discouraged. Rebecca knows that she will not be able to discourage Jamal from pursuing his plan.</td></tr>
<tr><td>2. B</td><td>Context Clues</td><td>The words hopes dashed and frown are clues that disheartened means depressed or sad.</td></tr>
<tr><td>3. B</td><td>Multiple-Meaning Words</td><td>Rebecca wants to "occupy the attention" (words from the definition) of Jamal in that she is "intrigued enough" (words from the passage) to hear his thoughts on how he plans to reach fame.</td></tr>
<tr><td>4. C</td><td>Plot</td><td>The information in paragraphs 8 and 9 suggest that Jamal's seeing the cupcakes gives him the idea to set a record for eating cupcakes.</td></tr>
<tr><td>5. D</td><td>Character</td><td>Rebecca is presented as a good friend, so "caring" is the best answer. Although Rebecca thinks Jamal's idea is wild, she listens, agrees to be his witness, and encourages him to try again after he fails.</td></tr>
<tr><td>6. A</td><td>Conflict</td><td>Jamal thinks it will be easy to set a world record, but he is wrong.</td></tr>
<tr><td>7. D</td><td>Personification</td><td>Humans and animals can leap, but not chocolate sprinkles.</td></tr>
<tr><td>8. C</td><td>Foreshadowing</td><td>"Or so he thought" indicates that Jamal may think he has found his answer, but he has not (which is shown in paragraphs 16 and 17, when Jamal fails).</td></tr>
<tr><td>9. A</td><td>Chronology</td><td>Right after Jamal eats the cupcakes (paragraph 15), he figures that he has not set a record (paragraph 17).</td></tr>
</table>

\"No Matter Where We've Been\"		
Answer	**Skill**	**Explanation**
1. D	Connotation	The Plains are described as fairly desolate except for wildlife. Saying that the prairie "crawls" with tarantulas is to say that there are many of them. "Abundant" is correct.
2. A	Hyperbole	Because the stars do not actually buzz, that image/phrase is an example of hyperbole.
3. A	Theme	The lines "I swore I'd never come home / to the Plains" and "no matter where I've been, / it's home" indicate that living life on the Plains is special because it's like no other place.
4. B	Conclusion/ Inference	The reader can tell from piecing together the information at the beginning and the end of the poem that the speaker left the Plains but returned.
5. C	Author's Organization	The poet organizes the poem by describing the stars, the wildlife, and the weather—among other things—that make the Plains a desirable place to the speaker.

		"Sizzling Hot Summer Camps"
Answer	**Skill**	**Explanation**
1. D	Details	The information in the section "Who Can Participate" indicates that July 18 is the last day.
2. B	Conclusion/ Inference	The information in the sections "What You Need" for all three camps indicates that the camps provide what the participants need.
3. C	Comparison/ Contrast	The "Kung Fu for Youth" Camp lasts from July 11 to July 15, so students who have only one free week can attend this camp.
4. A	Fact/Opinion	"It's the most fun you can have indoors" is the opinion of the author of the advertisement; this information cannot be proved.
5. D	Author's Purpose	The information in these sections provides both a picture of what students will do and some of the outcomes expected.
6. B	Author's Purpose	The passage is an advertisement, and the author likely has two purposes: to inform readers about the camps and, in doing so, persuade them to attend. The best answer of the four options is "inform readers about the camps that are available."

"Face Facts About Mount Rushmore"

Answer	Skill	Explanation
1. C	Prefixes	*Pan-* means "all," so "wide view" is the best answer.
2. D	Context Clues	The words *not scheduled to speak* are a clue that *spontaneously* means "without being planned."
3. A	Main Ideas	The section is mainly about how Robinson's original proposal was influenced by Borglum and President Coolidge.
4. D	Cause-Effect	The text specifically states that the Needles was rejected because Borglum believed the granite was brittle and the pillars were too thin to support the sculptures.
5. A	Fact/Opinion	Saying that Borglum's survey "clearly needed a closer look" is a judgment, the opinion of the author.
6. B	Author's Purpose	The section title is a hint that this section is a continuation of the article, which presents facts that the author thinks will be "intriguing" to readers; therefore, this section is intended to present more facts that the readers will likely find surprising.

"Bad Sports"

Answer	Skill	Explanation
1. A	Main Ideas	The last sentence in paragraph 1 and the second sentence in paragraph 6, as examples, clearly identify the author's position on this issue—she thinks youth sports are being taken too seriously.
2. B	Conclusion/ Inference	In paragraph 6, the author specifies what she sees as the benefits of playing sports.
3. D	Conclusion/ Inference	The image of three kids with their arms wrapped around one another's shoulders best conveys the idea of unity or respect for teammates.
4. D	Conclusion/ Inference	The question essentially asks for a paraphrase of the author's point in the sentence. Option D captures the idea aptly.
5. C	Author's Purpose	The author pulls in a statistic from a published source in order to lend credence to her argument that the majority of kids find organized sports unsatisfactory.

"Bad Sports" and "The Gym Class ~~Nobody~~ Somebody"

Answer	Skill	Explanation
1. D	Comparison/ Contrast: Tone	The author of "Bad Sports" is critical of the state of youth sports; the author of "The Gym Class ~~Nobody~~ Somebody" adopts a reflective tone when thinking back about events.
2. C	Comparison/ Contrast: Inference	Both authors convey that young people should enjoy sports. The endings of both passages reinforce this point.
3. A	Comparison/ Contrast: Inference	The author of "Bad Sports" talks about her observations of her children playing sports. "The Gym Class ~~Nobody~~ Somebody" is literary nonfiction, so it relates personal experiences.
4. B	Comparison/ Contrast: Inference	The first paragraph of "The Gym Class ~~Nobody~~ Somebody" contains details that point to feeling bored on the sports field.

The Gym Class ~~Nobody~~ Somebody

By Jake Kinnett

1   The Texas heat is the enemy. Sweat on my forehead rushes like a river to my eyes. Rubbing them doesn't lessen the stinging, but I cannot resist. Every day is the same in my eighth-grade gym class. I stand, unnoticed, in right field. I take off my baseball glove because I know I won't need it. I wait for class to be over the way a prisoner waits to be released. I wind the dial of my watch and tap on it, thinking the second hand has stopped moving.

2   But on this particular day, with 3 minutes and 42 seconds remaining, something happens that has never happened before. There is a fly ball heading my way and nobody else is near. At first I think that I am seeing things. Because the sun punishes us with blinding rays, it is quite possible that I am being deceived. It takes only the shouts of my teammates to know that I am not <u>delusional</u>. "Get under it, Jake," someone commands. "Don't be scared of it," someone else hollers. A baseball is indeed heading toward me— the too-tall, chubby, clumsy kid who, while respected on campus for guitar playing, is lost on the sports field.

3   And then the ball pauses in midair while I am transported back to the fourth grade. Setting: Playground. "I'm open," I yell at my football team's quarterback, Paul Herrera. But every quarterback knows not to throw the ball to the person who is consistently picked last, who is allowed to play only because the teacher is watching. So I know it is <u>improbable</u> that my hands will touch that ball. Sure enough, Paul tries desperately to <u>catch</u> the eye of another teammate. But they are all heavily guarded. No one ever guards me. The nearest opponent is three city blocks away.

4   Paul takes one more look down the field. I can hear Paul's thought: *If Hector or Mike has the slightest opportunity to receive this pass, I'll throw it to one of them rather than waste the play on Jake.* I know I have to persuade him otherwise. So I lock eyes with him. And I yell, louder this time, "I'm open." *Come on. Throw it to me,* I <u>implore</u> in my head.

5   That's when Paul does the unthinkable. He actually tosses the football directly, perfectly, gingerly to me. I do what I have seen my classmates do countless times before, but which I have never been given the opportunity on the school playground to do: I stick out my hands, grasp the ball, and pull it to my chest. I glance at Paul, and neither he nor I can believe I have caught it. Thirty yards separate me from a touchdown. So I run—fast. I travel nearly twenty yards before the others—stunned that I, Jake Hartman, have possession of the ball—can make their way to me. I have fewer than five yards to go when Terry, the steamroller, beelines it for me, grabs a fistful of shirt, and yanks. I hit the ground hard. The ball? It slips from my hands as though they were buttered. The shouts from my peers "Fumble. He fumbled!" redden my face and mock me the rest of the day.

6   Then the words "You've got this one, Jake" take me from football back to baseball. Again, I stick out my hands, ready to accept the ball that the bat was intent on delivering to me. It lands with a thud—in my ungloved hands—and it stays put. There is no way I can mess up this moment. There's no such thing as a fumble in baseball.

7   "Way to go, Jake" is the first cheer I hear. There are others—lots of them. In fact, I barely hear the coach's whistle, signaling the game is over.

8   As we head to the locker room, I keep admiring that baseball in my still-stinging hands. When I go to place it in the equipment locker, I run into Coach Wilson. "Nice catch," he says.

9   I look down at the mound in the metal ball basket. Then I ask, "Mind if I keep this one, Coach?" I figure one fewer ball in the equipment locker won't matter. But that ball does matter to me. A lot.

10   "No problem," he says, flashing a knowing smile and patting me on the back. I smile, too, pocketing my ball proudly.

11   For the rest of the day, my gloveless catch is big news. In math class, instead of doing their work, the guys entertain some girls by recounting the moment in a dramatic sportscaster's voice.

12   Now, this is the part of the story where I wish I could tell you that my status took roots. The truth is that the next day, when teams were being picked, I stood there, the best guitar player around, and was chosen—last. But having a desire to improve my ranking, I put on my glove, which covered up my watch, and I hustled to right field. Not even the intense Texas sun could keep me from watching the sky for a ball heading my way.

1. In paragraph 4, the word <u>implore</u> means to—

   A question
   B practice
   C wonder
   D plead

2. Which words found in paragraph 2 help the reader know what <u>delusional</u> means?

   A *has never happened before*
   B *I am seeing things*
   C *someone commands*
   D *lost on the sports field*

3. In paragraph 3, the word <u>improbable</u> means—

   A happening before
   B able to happen
   C likely to happen again
   D not likely to happen

4. Which word from paragraph 3 contains a root word that means "to carry"?

   A *transported*
   B *consistently*
   C *heavily*
   D *opponent*

5. Read the dictionary entry below.

   catch ['kach] v. 1. to take hold of or intercept (something falling, thrown, etc.) 2. to seize or capture, especially after a pursuit 3. to attract the attention of 4. to grasp the meaning of

   Which definition best matches how the word <u>catch</u> is used in paragraph 3?

   A Definition 1
   B Definition 2
   C Definition 3
   D Definition 4

6. The author uses the word <u>hustled</u> in paragraph 12 to show Jake's—

   A anxiety
   B confusion
   C enthusiasm
   D strength

7. Paragraph 2 is mostly about—

   A how a ball has been hit to Jake for the first time
   B how Jake finds his gym class to be boring
   C what Jake's teammates say to him
   D how gym class is almost over

8. According to the passage, what is Jake fiddling with while on the baseball field?

   A His glove
   B His watch
   C A football
   D A whistle

9. Which of these is the best summary of the passage?

   A While it is usually unexciting, gym class changes everything for Jake one day.
   B The heat and blinding sun usually make gym class miserable for Jake, but he promises not to let the conditions bother him when playing baseball.
   C For Jake, gym class is simply something that must be endured.
   D Gym class is wearisome for Jake and even brings back a bad memory, except when he achieves star status, even if only for one day.

10. On the playground in the fourth grade, Jake is thrown the football because—

    A   the teacher demands that all students get to play.
    B   he does not have far to run to make a touchdown.
    C   the quarterback cannot find anyone else who is open.
    D   the quarterback feels bad for picking him last.

11. In the passage, Jake changes from feeling—

    A   cowardly to brave
    B   unpopular to popular
    C   disinterested to interested in baseball
    D   hostile to friendly with his peers

12. The outdoor settings in the passage help to establish—

    A   why sports do not appeal to Jake
    B   why Jake prefers to be left alone
    C   how Jake feels when he is at school
    D   how Jake admires his athletic classmates

13. What is the conflict presented in paragraphs 3 and 4?

    A   Paul cannot understand what Jake is saying.
    B   Jake struggles to persuade Paul to give him a chance.
    C   The teacher forces Paul to pick Jake for his team.
    D   Jake does not think that Paul is a good quarterback.

14. The turning point of the passage occurs when—

    A   Jake catches the baseball
    B   Jake fumbles the football
    C   Jake talks to his coach
    D   Jake's teammates tell him what to do

15. Which statement expresses the theme of the passage?

    A   Appreciate the time you spend with your friends.
    B   In difficult situations, take a positive approach.
    C   Avoid taking on more responsibility than you can handle.
    D   In competitive sports, the most important thing is winning.

16. Read this sentence from paragraph 12.

    Now, this is the part of the story where I wish I could tell you that my status took roots.

    The figurative phrase "I wish I could tell you that my status took roots" means the narrator wishes—

    A   he developed an interest in gardening
    B   he became popular with girls
    C   his knowledge of baseball increased
    D   his glory as an athlete continued to grow

17. Which of these is an example of simile in the passage?

    A   *Sweat on my forehead rushes like a river to my eyes.*
    B   *It slips from my hands as though they were buttered.*
    C   *There's no such thing as a fumble in baseball.*
    D   *As we head to the locker room, I keep admiring that baseball in my still-stinging hands.*

18. In paragraph 1, the author uses the metaphor "The Texas heat is the enemy" to—

    A   establish the setting of the story
    B   reflect the narrator's fear of playing sports

C   state the central conflict of the story

D   express the narrator's feelings about his surroundings

19. Which of these is an example of personification in the passage?

   A   *Rubbing them doesn't lessen the stinging . . .*

   B   *. . . the sun punishes us with blinding rays . . .*

   C   *. . . only because the teacher is watching.*

   D   *I hit the ground hard.*

20. Which sentence from the passage contains an example of hyperbole?

   A   *The nearest opponent is three city blocks away.*

   B   *I glance at Paul, and neither he nor I can believe I have caught it.*

   C   *As we head to the locker room, I keep admiring that baseball in my still-stinging hands.*

   D   *I figure one fewer ball in the equipment locker won't matter.*

21. At the end of paragraph 1, the author uses an analogy to express the narrator's—

   A   desire to be accepted

   B   familiarity with ordinary experiences

   C   anticipation of the end of gym class

   D   lack of self-control

22. Which words signal the beginning of a flashback?

   A   *A baseball is indeed heading toward me . . .*

   B   *. . . I am transported back to the fourth grade.*

   C   *That's when Paul does the unthinkable.*

   D   *As we head to the locker room . . .*

23. What does the title of the passage foreshadow?

   A   The words the coach says to Jake

   B   The feeling Jake has on the football field

   C   The way Jake feels about playing sports

   D   The reaction Jake receives from his baseball teammates

24. Jake wants to keep the baseball most likely because it represents—

   A   gaining recognition from his peers

   B   exploring new interests

   C   receiving help from others

   D   accepting himself as he is

25. The mood in paragraphs 7 through 11 is best described as—

   A   peaceful

   B   serious

   C   relaxed

   D   celebratory

26. In the last paragraph, what does the author do to slow down the action?

   A   Switches tense and speaks directly to readers

   B   Uses persuasive language and credible evidence

   C   Shifts the point of view from first to third person

   D   Uses language that appeals to the senses

27. The author implies that Jake keeps the baseball he catches because—

   A   he forgets to place it in the equipment locker

   B   Coach Wilson understands the ball's significance to him

   C   he wants to show it to the girls in math class

   D   Coach Wilson wants him to practice playing baseball at home

28. What happens right after Paul throws the ball to Jake?

    A   Jake fumbles the ball.
    B   Jake hears his teammates' shouts.
    C   Jake runs to try to make a touchdown.
    D   Jake asks his coach if he can keep the ball.

29. What can the reader conclude from the teammates' comments in paragraph 2?

    A   They think of Jake as an important member of the team.
    B   They are not confident that Jake will make the catch.
    C   They don't understand why Jake isn't wearing his glove.
    D   They know the blinding sun is distracting to Jake.

30. What is similar about Jake's experiences playing football and baseball?

    A   His teammates cannot hear his calls.
    B   He plays in order to try to impress his peers.
    C   He does not feel visible to his teammates.
    D   He is not given the opportunity to prove himself.

31. Which excerpt from the passage reveals the author's opinion?

    A   . . . the too-tall, chubby, clumsy kid who, while respected on campus for guitar playing, is lost on the sports field.
    B   . . . I stick out my hands, grasp the ball, and pull it to my chest.
    C   I have fewer than five yards to go . . .
    D   I look down at the mound in the metal ball basket.

32. Which prediction about the narrator can be supported?

    A   Jake will try harder in gym class.
    B   Jake will be asked by his peers to play more often.
    C   Jake will receive an award from the coach.
    D   Jake will give up playing guitar for baseball.

33. Which sentence best shows a change in the narrator's attitude?

    A   Every day is the same in my eighth-grade gym class.
    B   I figure one fewer ball in the equipment locker won't matter.
    C   The truth is that the next day, when teams were being picked, I stood there, the best guitar player around, and was chosen—last.
    D   Not even the intense Texas sun could keep me from watching the sky for a ball heading my way.

34. The purpose of this passage is to—

    A   compare playing baseball to playing football
    B   encourage readers to participate in sports
    C   explain the value of playing baseball and football
    D   tell about one boy's experiences playing sports

35. The author develops this passage by—

    A   comparing and contrasting two sports
    B   switching back and forth in time
    C   relating the events in the order in which they occur
    D   relating information from most to least important

Demonstrating Understandings with Reading Activities

This section is designed with the principle that students need opportunities to demonstrate what they know and develop new understandings as strategic readers and thinkers, and that teachers need opportunities to introduce, review, and reteach reading skills and to assess what students know in order to build on their understandings.

The activities that compose this section are based on the most commonly assessed reading standards. Each activity includes some or all of these parts:

- An introduction or purpose statement
- Special resources (in addition to typical classroom supplies)
- A set of procedures
- A model
- An assessment
- An extension
- Student samples

The activities are print rich. They are easy for teachers to prepare for because they require only a few, easily accessed materials. The procedures are simple for teachers to follow and allow for flexibility. The assessments allow students to reflect on their thinking, their challenges, and their successes. Through these assessments, teachers can gain entrance to the students' thinking and can celebrate lightbulb moments and clarify and expand on lesser-formed ideas (Serafini 2004). Students are invited to work collaboratively to construct meaning (Vygotsky 1978), to think creatively, to problem solve, and to feel confident as learners.

135

The activities are also designed to fit in with the gradual release of responsibility model of instruction (Pearson and Gallagher 1983). That is, some activities will work well as introductions to reading skills, with the teacher introducing and defining terms and concepts and modeling the tasks. Other activities include only a short guided practice, because the standards involved are more familiar to students. That way, the majority of the time is spent allowing students to practice their skills with little teacher oversight; these activities are fairly open, allowing students to draw on other reading comprehension strategies that teachers have taught. Still other activities are planned specifically for the purpose of equipping students with strategies that they can access during reading assessments—such as building anchor examples and other tools that students can personalize for their use. No matter how teachers decide to incorporate these activities into their reading instruction, they are meant to be inviting, varied, interactive, thought provoking, and confidence boosting.

Contents

Activities for Vocabulary Development

Poetic Words	(Context Clues)
Context Clues Search	(Context Clues)
The Breakup	(Prefixes/Roots/Suffixes)
Word Power	(Connotation)

Activities for Important Ideas

Chunk and Jot Down	(Main Ideas/Comprehension)
Quick Find	(Details)
From Daily Print to Nightly News	(Summary)

Activities for Literary Elements

Character-logues	(Character)
How Was Your Day?	(Character)
Real People, Real Traits	(Character)
We Have a Problem—and a Solution	(Problem/Solution)
Found Poetry	(Theme)

Activities for Literary Techniques

All in One Book	(Various Literary Techniques)
"I Am" Metaphors	(Metaphor)
Pick Two, Any Two	(Personification)
Winning Hyperbole	(Hyperbole)
Really Bad Analogies	(Analogy)
I Had a Feeling	(Mood and Tone)
You've Got Style	(Style)

Activities for Interpretations

Jumbled, Messed-Up, Mixed-Up Texts	(Chronology)
"I Am" Inferences	(Conclusions/Inferences)
I See the Resemblance	(Comparison/Contrast)
Scrooge Meets Pollyanna	(Fact/Opinion)
Says and Feels	(Supporting Evidence)

Activities for Text Matters

What's the Purpose?	(Author's Purpose)
Matching Purposes	(Author's Purpose)
The Scavenger Hunt	(Author's Purpose/ Author's Organization)

Activities for Vocabulary Development

Context Clues

Poetic Words

Reading poems with students chorally is a great way to get them thinking about word meaning, because poets often make painstaking decisions about rhythm and word choice. Students might be surprised that they can employ context clue strategies even with short texts like poems.

Resource   Poetry book: Prelutsky, Jack. 1990. *Something Big Has Been Here.* New York: Greenwillow Books.

Procedure and Assessment   Prepare by reading the poems "I Met a Rat of Culture" and "My Mother Made a Meatloaf" from Jack Prelutsky's book *Something Big Has Been Here.* (These poems should contain several words that are unfamiliar to students.) Choose one poem and make a transparency of it.

Share the poem a few times—with you reading the poem aloud the first time as students follow along on a transparency, and then with the students reading the poem chorally.

Make an anchor chart of the types and examples of context clues found in Chapter 3. Using the teacher's guide that follows, lead a discussion by pointing out focus words one by one and asking students to share how they can use context clues to help them understand these words. Refer to the types/examples of context clues on your anchor chart as needed and review other strategies for determining the meanings of unfamiliar words.

Teacher's Guide

POEM "I MET A RAT OF CULTURE"

Possible Focus Words	Clues
culture	Clued through description throughout the poem
Proverbs	Clue word *poetry*, a type of writing/literature, so *proverbs* must be a related word
perspicacious	Clued through description of difficult subjects like *bionics* and *hydroponics*, so *perspicacious* must mean "wise"
Circled	Clue word *visited*
Operetta	Clued through definition (a type of song)
gavotte	Clued through definition (a type of dance)
versed	Clue word *authority*; clue words *within his brains*; antonym clue words *did not know*
sonata	Clued through description (music played on a violin); clue word *performed*
erudition	Clued through description throughout the poem and the word *culture* in the title, so *erudition* must be related to learning or sophistication

POEM "MY MOTHER MADE A MEATLOAF"

Possible Focus Words	Clues
distress	Clued through description; clue words *no success*
powerless	Clue words *no success*
assailed	Clue words *whacked* and *smacked*
impression	Clue words *without a nick*
chisel	Clued through description/definition (something that *chips* or *dents*)
unblemished	Clued through description; clue words *didn't make a dent*
beset	Clued through parts of speech: other verbs mean "attack"
manufacture	Clued through parts of speech: verb *building*
Synonyms for failure throughout poem	*met with no success, powerless, failed completely to suffice, couldn't faze, made no impression, didn't make a dent, stayed unblemished, didn't make a difference, simply stood its ground*
Use of verbs to describe attempts to cut	*whacked, smacked, assailed, worked, chipped, set upon, fired at, beset, trample*

Context Clues

Context Clues Search

Resource   Short texts

Procedure   Prepare by finding and copying various short texts that contain challenging words, such as science and history articles in textbooks. Also make a copy of the "Context Clues Search Results" sheet (provided in Appendix A) for each student.

Part One: Reviewing Context Clues

Ask students if they know the meaning of the word *enigma*. Call on any volunteers.

Ask students again if they know the meaning of the word *enigma* after displaying the following sentence:

The Nazca lines in Peru are an <u>enigma</u>.

Then display this sentence:

Even after years of study, these mysterious lines drawn in the sand defy scientific explanation.

Have students explain which clues in the second sentence help them know the meaning. (Possible answer: An enigma is a mystery or riddle. Clue words are *mysterious* and *defy scientific explanation.*)

Tell students that words have meanings because they "live" within a context. Within the context are clues that can help students understand what a sentence means, even if they don't already know the meaning of each individual word. Provide a chart of the types and examples of context clues (see Figure 3.1 in the section on context clues in Chapter 3).

Part Two: Searching for Context Clues

Distribute the "Context Clues Search Results" sheet (provided in Appendix A).

Have students work in groups to read the short texts and find unfamiliar words and the context clues that illuminate them. Discuss that they should find at least four words and should fill in a square for each word. Provide a model by filling in the parts for the word *enigma*:

> Title of Text: *Mysteries Around the World*
> Sentence containing unfamiliar word: *The Nazca lines in Peru are an <u>enigma</u>.*
> Context clues: *Even after years of study, these <u>mysterious</u> lines drawn in the sand <u>defy scientific explanation</u>.*
> Guessed meaning: *Something that cannot be figured out.*
> Dictionary meaning: *A puzzling or inexplicable occurrence or situation.*

Explain that students should use the context clue(s) they identify to take a stab at the meaning of the word ("Guessed meaning") before looking it up ("Dictionary meaning").

Assessment and Extension

Have groups share their words, context clues, and types of context clues that were found.

If students find one type much more often than others, challenge them to find a variety of types of context clues in their reading and continue to record examples.

Collect and review the examples periodically.

Repeat the activity to provide practice with using context clues to determine the meanings of other types of tested vocabulary, such as word parts and multiple-meaning words.

Prefixes/Roots/Suffixes

The Breakup

Segmenting words to identify prefixes, roots, and suffixes is a strategy that students can use on a reading assessment when approaching unfamiliar words that assess word parts.

Procedure

Prepare by copying and cutting apart four sets of "Breakup Cards" from the sheet provided in Appendix A. Cut out each box so that the words are separated from their meanings.

Begin by writing these word parts on the board:

in	*fract*	*ile*
re	*fract*	*ment*
	fract	*ion*
	fract	*ion*
	fract	*ion*
	frag	*ure*
	frag	

Ask students to combine the word parts to create six words. (Students should come up with *fracture, infraction, fragile, fraction, refraction,* and *fragment.*) Ask students to use the words to determine the meaning of the root words *fract* and *frag.* (Students should say "break" or something similar.)

Divide the class into four groups.

Ask groups to segment each of the words they've created by drawing a line between the word's parts. Provide an example by dividing the word *refraction* into three parts: *re / fract / ion.* Then explain that the word parts *re* ("again"), *fract* ("break"), and *ion* ("process of") help you know that *refraction* means "the process of breaking up again (light by the eye)."

Then have groups match the word card with the corresponding meaning card by using their knowledge of prefixes, roots, and suffixes.

Assessment and Extension

Ask groups to compare their matches.

Throughout the year, collect other words that have recognizable segments. When a sufficient number of new words have been collected, repeat this activity or play Memory, in which students turn over two cards at a time to match a word and its meaning.

Connotation

Word Power

Procedure

Prepare by making one copy of the "Connotation Squares" (provided in Appendix A) and cutting out the squares. Keep each group's set of cards separate from the others.

Write the word *connotation* on the board. Tell students that *connotation* refers to a word's suggested meaning or associations, often its emotional effect or impact, rather than its explicit meaning.

Ask students to compare these sentences:

> *My cousin's car is a classic.*
> *My cousin's car is a heap.*
> *My cousin's car is a wreck.*
> *My cousin's car is a rattletrap.*

Allow students to explain that all four sentences mean the car is old, but the word *classic* has a different connotation than the other three.

Explain that many words have either a favorable or unfavorable connotation. Tell students that authors choose words with a particular connotation to help readers understand the intended meaning.

Display the following information:

Favorable
- My neighbor is <u>curious</u>.
- The athlete is _____.

Unfavorable
- My neighbor is _____
- The athlete is <u>skinny</u>.

Ask students to fill in the blanks by suggesting an opposite way to express the same idea in the sentences provided. (Possible answers are *My neighbor is* nosy, prying, *or* a snoop and *The athlete is* slim, slender, *or* lean.)

Divide students into groups of three. Distribute a set of Connotation Squares to each group. Ask the groups to work together to sort the words as having usually a favorable or usually an unfavorable connotation. Supply dictionaries. Tell students to have a basic sentence in mind to test out each word to determine the connotation.

Assessment

Write the headings "Favorable" and "Unfavorable" on the board. Ask group 1 members to share how they sorted their words by taping them under the appropriate headings. Have the other students agree or disagree with group 1's decisions. When necessary, provide sample sentences to help students talk about the words. (For instance, students might not know the word *aged*. Provide this sentence to help them make their decision: "The Parmesan cheese was aged to perfection in Venice, Italy, before being shipped to our restaurant.")

Repeat this process with the remaining two groups.

Extension

Provide short texts, such as magazine and newspaper articles, and ask pairs of students to go on a hunt for words that the authors use that clearly have either a favorable or an unfavorable connotation.

Ask students to record the sentence, underline the focus word, and write a statement that tells about the connotation.

Activities for Important Ideas

Main Ideas/Comprehension

Chunk and Jot Down

Passages on reading assessments can be quite long. Because students need to refer to them in order to answer the items, they need a way to remember where certain major events or topics are located; otherwise, they might end up reading the entire passage again and again. Using the strategy of "chunk and jot down," as explained in detail in Chapter 4, students can learn to divide text into manageable chunks and to summarize important events with key words and/or pictures or expressive faces to remember important moments in the passage—all of which can be helpful when students refer to the passage later to track down an answer.

Resource   Short story: Cofer, Judith Ortiz. 1995. "An Hour with Abuelo." In *An Island Like You.* New York: Orchard Books.

Procedure   Prepare by making one copy of the "Story Windows" sheet (provided in Appendix B) for each student.

Tell students that as you read "An Hour with Abuelo," you will stop along the way and ask them to write a key word or phrase and/or draw a picture to express what is happening. Tell students that they can also use a "feeling face" to express how the main character is feeling in the story.

Distribute a copy of the "Story Windows" sheet and markers to each student.

Begin reading. (If desired, display the pages as you read.) After the first paragraph, stop to model an example of what students might place in their first story window. Draw a stick figure with a jagged line down it vertically to show fragmentation. On the left side of the stick figure, draw a grandfather in a bed, and on the right side, draw a stack of books. Have students fill in their first window.

Continue reading. Stop after every few paragraphs right before the action changes, or a total of three or four times per page. Decide in advance where to stop reading. As students fill in their windows, continue to model as needed. Throughout, keep a quick pace; spending too much time on any one story window could interfere with the students' ability to stay with the text.

After the first reading, begin reading the story a second time, pausing in the same places and allowing students to share what they have drawn and written in their own story windows to help them remember that chunk of text.

Assessment   At first students may take too much time thinking about what to write and draw, which might hinder comprehension. Some students might want to include too many ideas; some might write words or phrases that are too vague or unimportant. Listen to the responses as students share their story windows to gauge their understanding of the strategy and how well they recognize the purpose and usefulness of it. Guide them with tips and reminders to help them refine how they decide what to draw and write. Practice using a wide variety of texts. Then show students how to re-create their story windows within the margins of a test passage.

Because the goal of the strategy is to help students locate important text to answer test items easily, ask important questions about the story and determine if students can read their story windows to recall significant events. As students answer the questions, have them show and discuss which of their story windows helped them to remember. Students will further see the value of the strategy.

Student Sample   Eighth grader Bianca jotted down key words and created illustrations to capture her understanding of "An Hour with Abuelo." See the figure that follows.

FIGURE 1

Details

Quick Find

Detail items should be the easiest type of item for students, because the answers are explicitly stated or paraphrased in the passage. Still, students need strategies for tracking down the answer. In this activity, students will locate details by using text organizers (such as subheadings) and text features (such as sidebars, maps, and photos with captions); the previous strategy/activity, "Chunk and Jot Down," can also help students locate important information.

Resource   Information article from a magazine

Procedure   Prepare by finding an informational article that has several subheadings and other text features (or use "Face Facts About Mount Rushmore," provided in Section 3). Make a copy of the article for each student. Read the article and highlight important details. Then formulate simple questions so that the answers are the details you have highlighted.

Place students in small groups. Distribute a copy of the article, not highlighted or marked in any way, to each student. Students should *not* read the article.

Proceed immediately to posing the detail questions, one by one, that you have prepared. Instruct each group to find the information as quickly as possible. Award one point to the team of the group member who answers the question first.

After each question, ask the student with the answer to reveal his or her strategy for finding the answer. Emphasize how key words in the question can be matched to key words in the text organizers and text features to help students know where to go to find the correct answer.

Extension   Photocopy additional informational articles from various sources. Ask groups to find details that can be used to formulate questions.

Then have groups exchange their articles and questions. Groups should work together to find the answers to the detail questions formulated by other groups. Encourage discussion of their strategies for locating information.

Summary

From Daily Print to Nightly News

Resources School or local newspaper
Newscast via the Internet (optional)

Procedure Prepare by collecting a number of copies of the school or local newspaper. Find an interesting feature article. Also access a newscast via the Internet, if desired, and set up viewing equipment.

Display the article. Ask students to think about the most important information as you read it aloud. When finished, have student volunteers offer information that should be included in a summary of the article. Remind students that a summary should capture the main ideas and most important details while leaving out minor details. List the most important information and have the teacher or a student volunteer formulate a summary verbally.

In pairs students should comb through the newspapers to find two interesting articles and write summaries of them. Tell students that they will act as newscasters on the nightly news, and each person in the pair will read one of the summaries on the news program. As an option, first show a clip of a newscast and discuss the content, style, and so forth.

If desired, challenge students to write summaries that fit certain requirements. For instance, students might be challenged to write a summary that is only four sentences. Or they might be required to keep the summary to fewer than fifty words. Or they might try to include the answers to the journalistic 5W's (who, what, where, when, why) in one or two sentences.

Assessment Set up a mock news station with a table and two chairs at the front of the room. Begin the "broadcast" by allowing two pairs to deliver their summaries.

Then have the rest of the class—the viewers—discuss the strengths of the summaries. Ask these questions to prompt discussion:

- Do you have a complete picture of what happened?
- What information do you remember?
- Were minor details left out?

Repeat with the remaining pairs.

Activities for
Literary Elements

Character

Character-logues

Procedure   Prepare by making a transparency of the "Character Traits" list and the "Character-logue Sample" (provided in Appendix C).

Show the transparency of the traits list and ask a few student volunteers to share what they know about particular traits. (A student selecting *secretive* might say, "That means a person is hiding something.")

Tell students that they will be placed in pairs and will write a character-logue, which is a dialogue based on a character trait. To do so, they will use what they know about a trait—or use a dictionary to learn more about a trait—and write a conversation between two people in which one person expresses the characteristics of the trait in words and actions.

Display the "Character-logue Sample" and ask for volunteers to read/perform the parts. Then ask the rest of the class to offer traits that could appropriately fill in the blank. Students might offer *brave, courageous,* and *heroic.* List these traits and tell students that many traits are similar in meaning and can be grouped together appropriately within a certain context.

Place students into pairs, and ask them to write out their own character-logues that are similar in style and length to the sample.

Assessment   Allow the pairs to read/perform the character-logues. Have the class offer suggestions for the trait that is exemplified in the character-logue. When multiple answers are given and are appropriate, group them on the board (as done before).

Display the "Character Traits" list again and continue to group character traits that are similar in meaning. Remind students that on standardized tests, questions about characterization may use a variety of words to express a particular characteristic or quality of a story character or person.

Student Sample   Eighth grader Alix created a character-logue illustrating the trait *critical.* See the figure that follows.

FIGURE 2

> Character-logue
>
> Speaker 1: This store is so lame. Can we please leave?
>
> Speaker 2: No, I'm sure we can find something for the party here. Ooh look! This is perfect.
>
> Speaker 1: That's ugly. Why do you have such bad taste in clothing?
>
> Speaker 2: That was rude.
>
> Speaker 1: And also, those pants you bought earlier were awful. You seriously need to go faster. Hurry up.
>
> Speaker 2: Oh my gosh. Why are you so _____?
>
> answer: critical

Character

How Was Your Day?

Procedure   Prepare by making a transparency of the "Trait Description Outline" and "Trait Description for *Distant*" (provided in Appendix C).

Assign small groups of students a character trait from the "Character Traits" list (provided in Appendix C). (Select a recently studied trait or one with which you think students might be familiar.)

Display the "Trait Description Outline" transparency. Tell students to think of their character trait as a person and decide how that person might feel in a particular situation or setting.

To model, display the "Trait Description for *Distant*" transparency. Read it aloud. Then have student volunteers discuss how each line (the setting and the description/action) contributes to building an apt description of the character trait *Distant*.

Allow groups to fill in their outlines.

Assessment and Extension

Circulate to listen in on and contribute to the groups' discussions. If students need more information, refer to the dictionary or a recently read text that relates to the trait.

Allow groups to share what they have written about their trait.

If desired, display the "Character Traits" list and ask students to identify other traits that match their description. (Encourage students to make connections to traits that are not on the list as well.) For instance, students might discuss that the sample character traits description of *Distant* also fits the traits *aloof, detached, unemotional, standoffish, unapproachable,* and perhaps even *unfriendly.* Students might also use a thesaurus to enhance their discussion and understanding of similar traits. Being able to make associations among character traits will help students answer characterization items on reading assessments.

Create a class book of the groups' work. Add pages when books students read and discuss in class present opportunities to learn about new character traits.

Student Samples

Seventh graders know just how trait words feel. See the figures that follow.

My name is __Daring__ (character trait).

Today was a __exciting__ day.

Getting ready for school today,
I put my clothes on backwards because the principal forbids it.
During __math__ class,
I used cross multipling even though it's the teacher's pet peeve.
At lunch,
I started a food fight to get everyone dirty,
In the hallway,
I knocked down all the teachers on the way to my locker just to see what they do.
After school,
I jumped off the roof riding my skateboard because I wanted to outstunt somebody.
That is what life is like when you're __Daring__ (character trait).

FIGURE 3   Gunner and Abigail described a *daring* day.

My name is __Appreciative__ (character trait).

Today was a __full of thanks__ day!

Getting ready for school today,
I was happy my sister did not use all the hot water
During __math__ class,
I was pleased the test was canceled
At lunch,
I was glad I picked up the right sack lunch instead of my dad's because he eats jalapeño sandwiches.
In the hallway,
I was ecstatic to find my phone that I lost earlier.
After school,
I was joyful it was Friday!
That is what life is like when you're __grateful__ (character trait).

FIGURE 4   Erika recognized what it means to be *appreciative.*

Character

Real People, Real Traits

Resources   Biographies of interest at http://www.notablebiographies.com

Procedure   Prepare by making a transparency of the "Graphic Organizer About Lance Armstrong" (provided in Appendix C). Print the biography of Lance Armstrong as well as others of interest at http://www.notablebiographies.com.

Display the transparency of the graphic organizer, but do not discuss it. Begin reading aloud the biography of Lance Armstrong. At appropriate points, stop reading to show how the information from the biography is represented on the web. When finished, review the web again, making sure students understand that the information on the web is organized by pinpointing a trait or attribute and then providing an example.

Place students into small groups. Distribute the other biographies.

Photocopy for each group the "Character Traits" list (provided in Appendix C). Ask students to read their biographies, and as they do, think of character traits from the list that match how the author describes the person. Instruct students to use poster board and drawing supplies to create a web with traits/descriptions and examples as they read, similar to the one presented about Lance Armstrong.

Assessment   Allow students to present their webs to the class and discuss the traits and examples they included.

Student Sample   Seventh grader Kristopher read about Mae C. Jemison and created a web of her traits. See the figure.

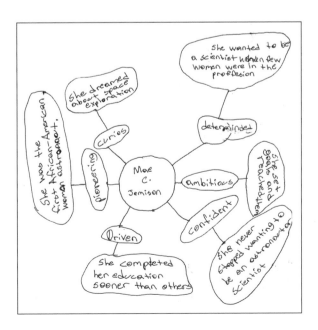

FIGURE 5

Problem/Solution

We Have a Problem—and a Solution

Resources   Grade-appropriate released test passages and items

Procedure   Prepare by finding and copying four test passages that are literary and feature a main character who has a problem and finds a solution. If the passages have associated items about the problem and/or solution, cut out these items and use them to make a transparency.

Place students in four groups. Distribute one of the test passages to each group. Tell students that they will be searching for the main character's problem and solution in the passage. If desired, ask students to practice the "chunk and jot down" strategy (described in Chapter 4) as they read the passage together.

After they have finished reading, ask students to write just one sentence that articulates the main character's problem and one sentence that captures the solution to the problem. Also ask students to underline the sentences in the passage that help readers know the story problem and solution.

Assessment and Extension   When students have finished working, ask the members of the first group to tell the class about the story they read. (If appropriate, ask students to use their notes from the "chunk and jot down" strategy to help them formulate their summary.) Then have these students read their problem sentence and their solution sentence.

Next, display the transparency that features the problem and/or solution item(s) for this passage. Ask the students in the group to read the item(s) and select the answer(s). Then discuss whether their sentences match the correct answers in the item(s) closely. (If they match, draw attention to the notion that the answers to test items are written succinctly and may not include all of the details that the students used.)

Conduct this same process with the remaining groups.

Then have all four groups discuss the supporting sentences they underlined that help readers determine the story problem and solution. Ask students to think about how authors present problems and solutions. (For instance, ask if the problem or solution was presented through dialogue, through description/action, etc. Was the problem or solution stated or did readers have to infer it?)

Also ask students to think about the structure of the narratives and about where the problems and solutions appear. (For instance, ask if the problem is presented at the beginning and the solution at the end. Which passages fit this structure and which do not? Is there a reason for presenting problems and solutions in certain ways?)

Build on these discussions throughout the year as students encounter texts that use a problem-solution organizational pattern.

Theme

Found Poetry

Resources   Literary nonfiction: Momaday, N. Scott. 1998. "The Indian Dog." In *The Man Made of Words: Essay, Stories, Passages.* New York: St. Martin's.

Procedure   Prepare by creating a display board on which a variety of themes are listed. These themes could be individualism, overcoming challenges, importance of family, working together, being strong in times of difficulty, and so on. You might also display the themes and examples featured in Chapter 5. Make a transparency of the story "The Indian Dog" as well as the "Found Poem" provided in Appendix C.

Begin by showing students the display board and discussing the meaning of each theme, providing as many real-life examples as needed to ensure that they understand every theme.

Transition by telling students that they will be writing poetry based on texts they read throughout the year. Explain to students that found poetry is the borrowing of words and phrases from a text and arranging the words, adding words, and deleting words in order to create a poem. Display and read "The Indian Dog," and then the sample found poem. Have students discuss how the theme of the original text is still present in the found poem example.

Then read a text as a class and have students use drawing supplies to create and illustrate their own found poetry that captures the theme.

Assessment and Extension   Host a poetry reading so that students can read their poems to the class. Allow students to discuss the theme of the text they read and their process for creating a found poem. Then have students attach their poems beneath the appropriate theme on the display board. (Students should add new themes as needed.)

On other occasions as students read texts with other themes, ask them to contribute found poetry to the display board.

Activities for Literary Techniques

Various Literary Techniques

All in One Book

The first stage of practice with literary techniques is often to isolate them for students, talk about their qualities, and then assign students to create their own examples. It is much more difficult to be aware of the presence of literary techniques when they are not isolated in some way by a teacher or worksheet. In this activity, students have the opportunity to demonstrate what literary techniques are at their fingertips, so to speak, as they read poetry and attempt to uncover examples; this activity also is likely to bring forward the techniques that require more review.

Resources   Poetry collection: Nye, Naomi S. 2000. *Come With Me: Poems for a Journey.* New York: HarperCollins.

Procedure   Prepare by making copies of the following poems by Naomi Nye so that when the class is divided into groups of three or four, each group will have a copy of every poem: "Come with Me," "Observer," "Where Are We Going?," "Spinning," "Secrets," "Courage," and "Somebody's Story."

On the board, write the following words: *simile, metaphor, personification, hyperbole, figurative language.* (Explain that for the sake of this activity, *figurative language* refers to nonliteral or idiomatic uses of language that are not examples of the other categories.)

Tell students to work in their groups to read each poem and find the examples of the literary techniques indicated on the board. Ask groups to assign a note taker to write down what they find. Encourage students to scour the poems to find as many examples as they can; remind them that more than one kind of literary technique will likely be found in each poem. Select one poem and model, if needed.

Assessment   Allow volunteers to share the examples they have located for each poem.

Use the "Teacher's Guide" that follows to verify the examples as well as identify additional examples of literary techniques that groups might not have noticed.

Using the sheet in Appendix D titled "Anchor Examples for Literary Techniques," have students choose anchor examples by filling in a definition and examples for the literary techniques discussed in this activity.

Teacher's Guide

"Come with Me": *quiet minute between two noisy minutes, waiting, tucked under the wing of the day* (personification)

"Observer": *cloud sweeps* (personification)

"Where Are We Going?": *city that glitters* (figurative language); *thinking signs* (personification)

"Spinning": *you stand upright like another kind of animal* (simile); *the days have steps in them, slopes and curves* (personification); *first grade takes twenty years to get through* (hyperbole); *second grade only takes ten [years to get through]* (hyperbole); *the rivers inside your body* (figurative language); *are you a spinning wheel in space* (figurative language or metaphor); *hooked . . . to the Arctic Sea* (figurative language)

"Secrets": *suitcase filled with tiny unspoken tales* (figurative language); *a secret is a ticket* (metaphor)

"Courage": *word has tough skin* (personification); *a word must slide and sneak and spin* (personification); *a word is brave* (personification)

"Somebody's Story": *in a voice as clear as a penny and a dime* (simile); *came to be as tall as a riddle, as full as a shadow, as far as the wind* (similes); *a sleep as deep as desert sand* (simile); *my dreams were the stories that crossed the land* (metaphor [dreams were stories] and personification [stories crossed the land])

Metaphor

"I Am" Metaphors

For students who have trouble with identifying metaphors in texts, writing an extended metaphor about themselves (or another person or object/concept) could help them to see that metaphor is a direct comparison—*I compared to something else*. A memorable comparison provides students with an anchor example that they can recall when encountering items about metaphor on a reading assessment.

Procedure   If desired, begin with a review of metaphor, perhaps collecting examples from texts that have been recently shared with the class.

Tell students that they will write about themselves in order to create a metaphor. Provide the following list on the board and add to it as a class.

I am a baseball legend in my own mind.
I am a night owl.
I am a speed demon on my roller blades.
I am a tornado on the football field.

Model the task, as shown in the following section. Then provide paper and drawing supplies so that each student can write an extended metaphor and illustrate it.

Model   Display and discuss these examples:

- I am a walking encyclopedia. I am filled with information of all kinds. Just ask me!
- I am an eighth-grade caterpillar. All year long I am in the cocoon of middle school. At the end of the year, I develop wings and fly away to become a high school butterfly.

Assessment and Extension   Have students share their work with the class, reteaching as necessary.

Emphasize the distinction between simile and metaphor by asking students to discuss how their metaphors can be turned into similes.

Using the "Anchor Examples for Literary Techniques" sheet in Appendix D, have students choose anchor examples by filling in the definitions and examples for similes and metaphors.

Personification

Pick Two, Any Two

Personification often hinges on attributing a human quality or action (the verb) to a nonhuman or abstract thing (the subject). Students should be able to scrutinize the subjects and verbs of sentences in order to recognize personification. A memorable anchor example will help students when encountering personification items on a reading assessment.

Procedure   Display these examples of personification and read them aloud:

- The stars refused to show up for work last night.
- The tree rejected the tree house by strangling it with its heavy branches.

Ask volunteers to explain why the sentences are examples of personification. (Possible answers: *Stars can't refuse to show up; tree branches can't strangle anything.*) Help students see that the verbs are actions that can be attributed to humans only, not nonhuman things.

Show a transparency of the "Nonhuman Subjects and Human Verbs" sheet (provided in Appendix D).

Ask pairs of students to write and illustrate an example of personification by selecting one subject and one verb and then adding more description.

Assessment   Ask volunteers to read their examples of personification. Have other students comment on why the statement is an example of personification.

Using the "Anchor Examples for Literary Techniques" sheet in Appendix D, have students record their anchor example by filling in the definition and example for personification.

Hyperbole

Winning Hyperbole

Procedure　Prepare by making a transparency of the Appendix D sheet "Excerpt from Carl Sandburg's poem 'Yarns.'" Also make a copy of the "Hyperbole Starters" sheet (provided in Appendix D) for each student.

Show students the poem excerpt and ask them to read along with you. Have students share what they notice. Build on the response that the events are exaggerated. Tell students that exaggeration in literature is called hyperbole.

Distribute the copies of "Hyperbole Starters." Discuss the example in the first row. Tell students that the second sentence is an example of hyperbole that builds on the first sentence; talking about a movie nonstop for two days is an exaggeration that helps you know how much Marissa loved the movie.

Ask students to work individually to read the sentences in the first column and add a sentence in the second column that creates an example of hyperbole. Tell students to be creative in order to create memorable images.

As students are working, circulate to answer their questions. Use the "Teacher's Guide for Hyperbole Starters" (provided in Appendix D) to help students understand their task, if necessary.

Assessment　Write these categories on the board: Silliest; Most Serious; Laugh-Out-Loud Funniest; Scariest/Spookiest; Most Creative; Most Descriptive.

Have students in small groups compare their work within their groups and nominate the hyperbole sentence that is the best in each category listed on the board.

When groups are finished deciding, ask each group to read aloud its nominee for the first category. Discuss the examples, and have the class vote for the best one. (The teacher should break any ties or declare the winner if all groups vote loyally for their own example!) Continue until a winner in all categories is awarded.

Using the "Anchor Examples for Literary Techniques" Appendix D sheet, have students record their anchor example by filling in the definition and example for hyperbole.

Student Samples　Because the students in a seventh-grade class created many wonderful examples of hyperbole, selecting the winners for each category was tough. The figures that follow show some of the winning examples.

FIGURE 6 Alison was selected by her peers as the student who created the silliest example of hyperbole.

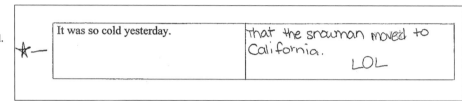

My backpack has so much stuff in it.   Silliest   I could open a small Walmart in there.

FIGURE 7 Chandler's example of hyperbole made her classmates laugh out loud.

It was so cold yesterday.   That the snowman moved to California.   LOL

FIGURE 8 Elizabeth took the prize for being the most creative with her example of hyperbole.

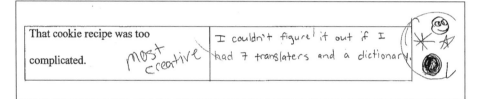

That cookie recipe was too complicated.   most creative   I couldn't figure it out if I had 7 translaters and a dictionary.

Analogy

Really Bad Analogies

Anchor examples are those that students can create and memorize to help them access certain types of literary techniques items on standardized tests. Usually the goal is for students to create a representative, easy-to-memorize, *good* example of a literary technique. In this activity, however, students create analogies that are really *bad*—but no less memorable, and perhaps even more so. An anchor example of a bad analogy is equally useful come test time!

Procedure

Part One: Explanation of the Term

Tell students that an analogy is a comparison of similarities between two things that are usually dissimilar. To illustrate this definition (because students might be scratching their heads in confusion), display this example from Andrew Clements's *Frindle* (a text many students might have read a few years ago):

> *Nick could feel a homework assignment coming the way a farmer can feel a rainstorm.*

Explain to students that Nick, a boy at school, is not likely to have much in common with a farmer, but in this analogy, they are alike: Both know something is about to happen.

Say that writers use analogies to help readers understand a new situation by comparing it to something that is more familiar to them. Answer questions or provide more examples if needed.

Part Two: Practice

Display the Appendix D sheet titled "Really Bad Analogies."

Tell students that the analogies are from a contest the *Washington Post* held for the worst analogies people could write (as part of its long-running humor contests). Read the analogies and discuss them. Draw attention to how two unalike things are described as being similar. Let students share their reactions to the analogies that are gross, laugh-out-loud funny, or just plain bizarre.

Place students in pairs. Announce that the pairs are to write their own analogy that might be *bad* enough to win a *Washington Post* worst analogies contest.

Give students some subjects/topics to get them started with their analogy or have them comb through various texts to find analogies that interest them. Some general suggestions, from which students can think of specific images, include a young kid's ballet performance, my mother's hair every morning, and a mall the day after Thanksgiving.

As a class, write a bad analogy together before moving on to working as pairs. If desired, use the first part of any of the bad analogy examples and ask the class to come up with an original comparison to complete it. Draw attention to the words that link the two parts of the analogies, such as *the way . . . , like . . . , or about as often/well as . . . (That lawyer speaks the truth about as often as a slob stays neat).*

Assessment

Have the pairs line up around the room. Ask the first pair to read their really bad analogy. Then ask the second pair to read their analogy. Allow these pairs (and the other classmates) to discuss each analogy, and then have their peers determine which of the two could be a winner in the worst analogies contest. The winning pair should stay standing, and the other pair should return to their seats.

Proceed down the line in this way until the last pair standing is declared the best of the worst analogies.

Using the "Anchor Examples for Literary Techniques" Appendix D sheet, have students record their anchor example by filling in the definition and example for analogy.

Mood and Tone

I Had a Feeling

Procedure   Display these sentences:

I am sorry.
I am sorry.
I am so shocked.
I am so shocked.

Tell students that if they emphasize the underlined word when saying each sentence, they will create a different mood. Ask for four volunteers to say the sentences and describe the moods (for example, apologetic, argumentative, sad, surprised).

Explain that mood and tone are important considerations for authors. The mood is the general atmosphere that the author creates using story elements (such as setting and plot). The tone is the author's attitude toward the subject matter he or she is writing about (such as taking a critical tone in an editorial).

Create and display a transparency of the "Moods and Tones" sheet provided in Appendix D.

Divide students into small groups. Provide each group with a variety of reading materials, such as newspapers (especially feature articles and editorials), poems, chapter books, and biographies. Also distribute sticky notes and pens.

Ask students to read the materials to find examples of matches for the moods and tones listed on the transparency (and/or suggest others that should be added to the list). Instruct students to mark the source with a sticky note and identify the mood or tone.

Assessment   As groups share their examples, collect observations about mood and tone. Pay particular attention to how authors use specific words (through descriptions, through settings, through dialogue, and so forth) to create a mood and establish a tone.

Using the "Anchor Examples for Literary Techniques" Appendix D sheet, have students record their anchor examples by filling in the definitions and examples for mood and tone.

Extension   Have students create a "mood album" by selecting a mood and finding images from magazines and lines from literature that evoke that particular mood. (Make sure that students tackle different moods so that the finished album includes variety.)

Style

You've Got Style

Starting in middle school, usually, and continuing through high school, reading assessments include items (both multiple choice and constructed response) that ask students to think about style, usually defined as the way in which authors craft text. These items can involve simply identifying a stylistic technique or, requiring much more skill, involve articulating the effect that the use of a stylistic technique has on a text. In this activity, students have the opportunity to analyze excerpts from a text in order to uncover what the author is doing with language, punctuation, and sentence structure as well as the effect the author is trying to achieve.

Procedure   Prepare by making five copies of the "Style Excerpts" and "Style Descriptions" sheets (provided in Appendix D).

Divide students into five groups. Distribute the "Style Excerpts" sheet, one per group.

Announce to students that the sheet includes twelve excerpts from Jerry Spinelli's (2007) *Eggs*. Tell students that they need not have read the book. Instruct students to read each excerpt and use their pens and paper to make notes about the author's use of style.

Display these focus questions and discuss them:

- Is the author using <u>sentence structure</u> in an unusual or interesting way?
- Is the author using <u>punctuation</u> in an unusual or interesting way?
- Is the author using <u>language</u> in an unusual or interesting way?

Allow students to begin working. Listen in on students' conversations.

After a few minutes, having given students a chance to read through and discuss several excerpts, distribute a copy of the "Style Descriptions" sheet to each group. Also provide scissors and tape.

Tell students that you are providing them with the "answers," and that their job is to match each excerpt to a style description. Ask students to cut apart the squares on both sheets. When students have found a match, they should tape the squares next to each other on a sheet of paper.

Assessment   Call on groups to share the excerpts they have matched to the descriptions. Discuss by using the "Teacher's Guide for 'You've Got Style'" (provided in Appendix D). Be sure to ask groups to point out the specific examples/sentences in the excerpts that meet the descriptions (for example, the fragments, the repetition, the questions).

Extension   Extend students' ability to notice features of style by having them read nonfiction works and hunt for noteworthy examples of author's craft and style. For instance, students might think about leads of nonfiction articles and discover the use of questions (and answers), a description of a problem or scene, an attempt to shock the reader with surprising facts, and so forth. Other stylistic features of nonfiction might include speaking directly to the reader, repeating a phrase or sentence for effect, and putting quotations around words to show that they are being used purposefully in an unusual way.

Collect these features on chart paper and add to them as students read nonfiction texts as a class.

Activities for Interpretations

Chronology

Jumbled, Messed-Up, Mixed-Up Texts

Resources   Picture book: Ahlberg, Allan. 2007. *Previously*. Cambridge, MA: Candlewick.

Procedure   Start by reading the picture book *Previously*. After a few pages, ask the students to identify the clever pattern that the author is using. (Students should be able to recognize that the story is being told in reverse through the use of the word *previously*.) When finished reading, discuss the importance of chronology in fiction. (Students should share that an identifiable chronology helps readers make sense of the important plot events.) Ask students how readers make sense of nonfiction texts. (Students might respond that associating main ideas with details helps readers. Discuss other responses.)

Divide the students into four groups. Announce to students that they will be working with both a fiction text and a nonfiction text. Tell students that their problem is that the sentences of the texts have been jumbled, and their job is to put each text back together again in a logical way—by sequencing the sentences of the fiction text and by using their knowledge of main ideas and details to reconstruct the nonfiction text.

Make four copies of the sheets "Jumbled Fiction Sentences" and "Jumbled Nonfiction Sentences" (provided in Appendix E) and distribute one of each sheet to every group. Also provide the groups access to scissors, poster board or thick paper, and tape.

Instruct the groups to cut out the jumbled sentences of the fiction and nonfiction texts, keeping them separated. Tell students to arrange the sentences in a logical way, and then tape the sentences to the poster board or thick paper. Repeat with the remaining set of sentences.

Assessment   When all groups have completed the two tasks, ask a representative from each group to display their work for the fiction text. Allow students to note any differences among the arrangement of sentences. Also have groups discuss the clues that helped them determine how to best reconstruct the text. (An answer key has been provided in Appendix E to help foster the discussion.) Students should note that the reader needs to be introduced to a main character first, that the character's past experiences are explained before transitioning to the present experiences, and so forth.

Repeat this process to discuss the nonfiction text. Students should note that the paragraph begins with a general statement and then is supported with facts and examples, questions are followed by answers, and transitions and dates help the reader keep track of the events across time.

Conclusions/Inferences

"I Am" Inferences

Procedure

Part One: Charades

On the board, make a two-column chart with the column headings "What I Know" and "What I Can Infer."

Explain the procedure for a version of charades that you will host. Tell students that you will act out a common, everyday action or movement. For example, tell students that if you put your finger over your lips, they can infer that you are asking them to quiet down. Instruct students to raise their hands when they know what you are doing. Tell students that they should first describe what you are doing (for example, "My teacher put her finger over her lips") and then say what can be inferred from the action (for example, "My teacher wants the class to be quieter").

As students respond, write the action descriptions under "What I Know" and their inferences under "What I Can Infer." (Remind students that they make inferences when they use what they see, read, and know in order to draw a conclusion about something.)

The chart that follows gives some example actions to act out (left side) and anticipates what inferences students might make (right side).

What I Know	What I Can Infer
My teacher put on a jacket.	My teacher is cold (or is going outside where it is cold).
My teacher yawned.	My teacher is sleepy (or tired or bored).
My teacher is limping.	My teacher's foot is hurt.
My teacher is holding her head in her hands.	My teacher has a headache (or is upset about something).
My teacher is shaking her hand and rubbing it.	My teacher's hand fell asleep.

Part Two: "I Am" Inferences

Divide students into small groups. Tell students that they will create "I Am" descriptions of something without identifying the thing by name. Give students suggestions for something they might describe—a favorite food, a particular job, an article of clothing, a nursery rhyme, and so forth. Remind students to use the five senses to describe the thing.

Display the following example by showing only one line at a time and pausing after each line to elicit guesses.

> *I prefer to do my work in nice weather, but even rain won't stop me.*
> *I handle all kinds of messages—some good, some bad.*
> *I am not afraid of an occasional paper cut.*
> *I watch for dogs, because most do not like my coming around.*
> *I am able to carry a large bag on my shoulders and back.*
> *I am . . .*

Students should guess that the example describes a mail carrier. Ask students how each line supports that inference.

Have students work in groups to select their mystery thing and write a description. Remind students not to reveal the name of their thing in the description itself.

Assessment   Ask students to share their work with the class by reading one line at a time and allowing their classmates to guess. Discuss how the descriptions provided information that helped them make the inferences.

Extension   Throughout the year, focus on specific aspects of texts that help readers make inferences. One topic could be dialogue tags. List dialogue tags that students have likely seen in literature and ask students to think about the inferences that can be made. The following chart provides examples:

Dialogue Tag	Possible Inferences
he exclaimed	Strong reaction, perhaps surprise, excitement, or shock
Marissa said, rocking back and forth and wringing her hands	Negative feeling, such as nervousness or in need of comfort
he said, his face beaming	Positive feeling, such as joy
she said, finally breaking the silence	Negative feeling, such as awkwardness between two or more people

Comparison/Contrast

I See the Resemblance

Resources   Paired passages (from released tests or other text sources)

Procedure   Prepare by finding two passages or texts that are similar in subject or theme. (Because this is a whole-class activity, all groups should work with the same passages or texts.) Make copies, either one per group or one per student. Also make copies, enough for one per group, of the "Things to Compare in Fiction Passages" sheet and/or the "Things to Compare in Nonfiction Passages" sheet (provided in Appendix E), depending on the types of passages you assign students to read.

Divide students into four groups, and distribute copies of the passages or texts.

Display a Venn diagram. Tell the students that after reading the two passages or texts, they will work in their groups to try to record more similarities and differences than any other group.

Read the passages or texts as a class. Use the opportunity to reinforce the "chunk and jot down" strategy (described in Chapter 4). Stop at various points to allow students to record and discuss their margin notes as they use this strategy.

Distribute the appropriate "Things to Compare" sheet(s) to the groups, and review the information. Also provide access to poster board and markers.

Ask students to work in their groups to record the similarities and differences between the two passages or texts, using their "chunk and jot down" margin notes and the information on the "Things to Compare" sheet(s) to guide them.

Assessment   Have one group display their poster board and "teach" the other students about the information they recorded. Prompt the group members to tell how they came up with their findings and where they can be found in the passages or texts.

Continue this process so that each group has a chance to talk about their work.

Gear the discussion so that students notice those aspects that some groups focused on but others did not. Help students draw distinctions between small ideas (details) and larger ideas (themes) that were noticed and recorded. Also, ask students to comment on the ways in which the "chunk and jot down" strategy helped them locate and glean similarities and differences.

Extension   Provide opportunities for students to compare various types of texts—for example, fiction with fiction, fiction with biography, expository writing with poems. Continue to help students increase their ability to recognize the "big ideas" that are worthy of comparison in the passages or texts, as these are usually the focus of comparison/contrast items for paired passages on reading tests.

Fact/Opinion

Scrooge Meets Pollyanna

Procedure

Part One: Strategy Lesson

Tell students that on a reading test, they are likely to encounter a question that asks them to distinguish fact from opinion. (Review definitions, such as a fact is true and can be verified, whereas an opinion is open for debate.) Tell students that one strategy for detecting an opinion is to determine whether the statement has a neutral meaning (usually a fact) or has a positive or negative meaning (usually an opinion). Display these statements:

Louis "Satchmo" Armstrong was born on August 4, 1901.

My teacher is great at writing poems.

Ask students to discuss which statement is an opinion that expresses an idea in a positive or negative way.

Then ask students to convert the positive opinion into a negative opinion. Elicit responses. (Students should offer, for example, "My teacher is not good at writing poems" or "My teacher is bad at writing poems.") Tell students that opinions can usually be changed from positive to negative and vice versa, which can help further distinguish opinions from facts.

Part Two: Strategy Practice

Divide the class into two groups. Assign one group to be "Scrooges" and one group to be "Pollyannas." Tell students that Ebenezer Scrooge, a character in Charles Dickens's novel *A Christmas Carol*, had a negative outlook on life. Explain that Pollyanna, on the other hand, a character in a children's novel by Eleanor H. Porter, always looked for the bright side of things.

Display these topics:

Camping
Going to the movies
Spending time with the family
Volunteer work
Homework
Extracurricular activities
Playing video games
Recycling
Competing/competition

Ask the Scrooges to write one statement for each topic that expresses an opinion in a negative way. Ask the Pollyannas to write one statement for each topic that expresses an opinion in a positive way.

Share and discuss these examples on the topic of baseball practice:

Scrooge: Baseball practice is nothing but quarter-sized mosquitoes biting at my ankles while I wait alone in right field.

Pollyanna: Baseball practice is a time to get together with friends on a beautiful sunny day.

Have the groups record their statements on one sheet of paper.

Assessment

Ask the groups to line up against opposite walls and face each other.

Announce the first topic—camping. Ask a member from each group to go to the front of the room and read the statement that relates to the topic. Have the opposite group members listen carefully for the opinion words that reflect either a positive or negative meaning. Discuss how listeners can determine whether the statement is by a Scrooge or a Pollyanna.

Then move on to the next topic and ask a different member of each group to read the prepared statements. Continue until all Scrooge and Pollyanna opinion statements have been shared.

Student Samples

The Pollyannas were positively upbeat, whereas the crankiness really came out in the Scrooges of a seventh-grade class, as can be seen in the figures that follow.

FIGURE 9

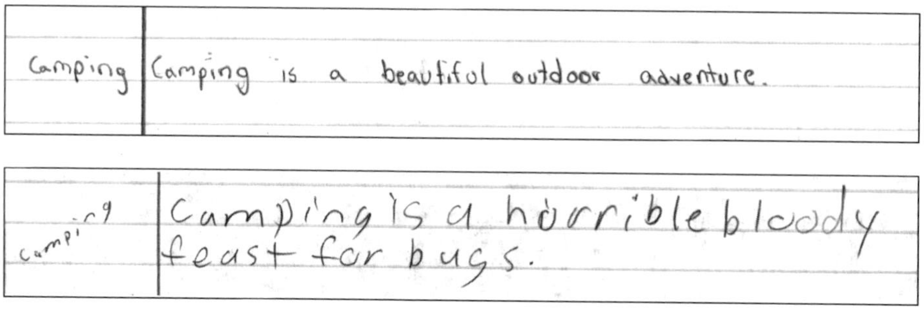

Camping	Camping is a beautiful outdoor adventure.

...g Campi	Camping is a horrible bloody feast for bugs.

FIGURE 10

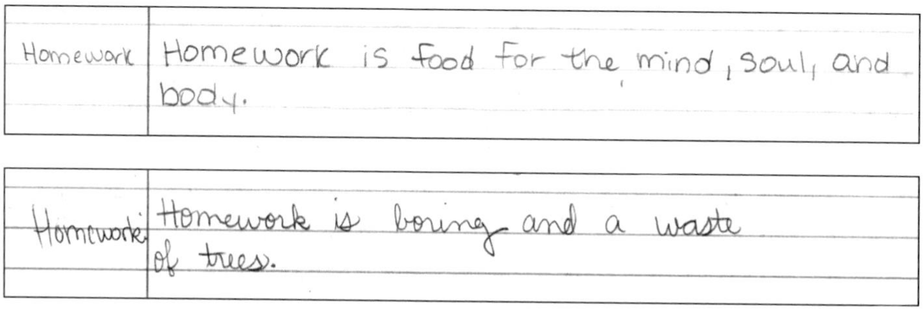

Homework	Homework is food for the mind, soul, and body.

Homework	Homework is boring and a waste of trees.

FIGURE 11

competition	I love a good challenge, it makes me work hard

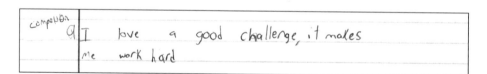

	Our team is going to lose so whats the point of even going. } competing/ competition

Supporting Evidence

Says and Feels

Supporting evidence (or textual evidence) items on reading assessments essentially task students to support a conclusion or big idea with specific evidence from the passage. Usually the correct answer is the idea or sentence that stands out in a meaningful way rather than some insignificant detail. In this activity, students pay attention to dialogue and connect it to an appropriate character trait. Doing so provides practice with the kind of thinking they will be required to do in order to answer supporting evidence items.

Procedure　　Prepare by making five copies of the "Says and Feels" sheet (provided in Appendix E). Cut out the boxes on each sheet, separating the dialogue statements from the character traits. Make five sets of the dialogue statements and character traits (shuffled so it's not obvious which statement matches which trait).

Tell students that in literary texts, authors require readers to make inferences based on what characters say and do. Provide an example by reading the following sentence from Joan Bauer's (1998) *Rules of the Road*:

Jus wanted to see you, honey. I meant to call.

Ask students if they can infer how the character saying those words might be feeling. Elicit responses. Then explain that the lines are spoken by a father who has a distant relationship with his daughter. Help students see that the words "I meant to call" are inference clues to how the character feels, which is regretful or apologetic. Tell students that on reading assessments, they will be asked to link an inference (sometimes about how a character is feeling) to an excerpt from the passage that supports that inference.

Place students in five groups. Give each group a set of the "Says and Feels" boxes. Then tell the groups to work together to infer which lines of dialogue correspond with which feeling/trait words. Ask students to be prepared to talk about the clues that help them know that a particular feeling/trait word is supported by an excerpt.

Assessment　　When students have finished working, ask the groups to listen as you read the first dialogue statement. Then call on a group to provide the feeling/trait word it selected for the statement. Ask the group to discuss the clues used to connect the feeling/trait word and the excerpt. Check with the other groups to see if they agree with the match. (The statements and feeling/trait words are correctly matched on the "Says and Feels" appendix sheet that you copied in order to make the sets.)

Continue in this fashion, calling on a different group each time, until all dialogue statements are discussed.

Extension   Have the class decide on a particular setting, such as summer camp or a sporting event. Then ask students to work individually to invent one line of dialogue for that setting and write it on an index card. On the back of the card, have students place the character feeling/trait that they think can be inferred from the line of dialogue. (If desired, display the "Character Traits" list provided in Appendix C.)

Illustrate the process by sharing this example:

(front of index card) "I know that I've been taking swimming lessons for two weeks, but I still don't think I'm ready to jump in without a life jacket."	*(back of index card)* RELUCTANCE

Ask students to discuss the clues that help them infer that the feeling/trait is *reluctance.* (Possible answer: "I still don't think I'm ready . . .")

When students finish creating their cards, allow them to work in small groups to read the lines of dialogue, find inference clue words, and decide the feeling/trait that can be inferred. Have them check their responses with the words written on the backs of the cards.

Let groups trade sets of cards until they have read and discussed them all.

Student Samples   Students in a seventh-grade class decided to create statements that might be heard while living life at sea. See the figures that follow.

I clenched my teeth. I couldnt believe Lucy didnt vote for me to be captain.	Furious

FIGURE 12   Jasmine knew clenching one's teeth is a sign of being *furious.*

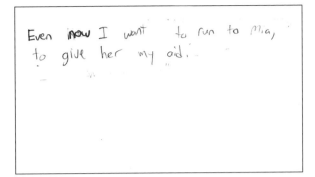

Even now I want to run to Mia, to give her my aid.

longing

FIGURE 13 Tyler pictured *longing* as wanting to run to help someone.

"Can you hear the waves in the distance? It's so calm, like there's never any problems out here."

~~envious~~
content

FIGURE 14 Elizabeth thought waves were calming, causing one to feel *content*.

Activities for Text Matters

Author's Purpose

What's the Purpose?

Students will recognize in this activity that a topic can be written about for many purposes and that word choice is often a key to identifying an author's purpose. On a reading assessment, students can access an author's purpose item by paying attention to the author's use of language as well as the text type and organizational structure.

Procedure The "Purposes and Examples" sheet (provided in Appendix F) features author's purpose words (left side) that often appear on reading assessments and examples of text that fit with each purpose (right side).

Make four copies of the sheet, cut apart the twelve boxes, and scramble them. Make four sets this way.

Divide students into four groups. Distribute a set of purposes and examples to each group. Ask groups to match the purpose word with the corresponding example.

Assessment Call on various groups to tell which example they matched to each purpose word you announce. Then have students identify the key words that helped them determine which purpose and example fit together. The words underlined in the following version of the sheet might be selected and discussed by groups; if not, lead a discussion to draw attention to these words.

Describe	Camp Townsend is located on the banks of a <u>sparkling blue</u> river and <u>nestled</u> between <u>two beautifully wooded</u> mountains.
List	Each camper is responsible for <u>the following: snacks and water, hiking boots, a fishing pole, a backpack, and a sleeping bag.</u>
Persuade/Convince	You <u>must</u> join us this weekend; <u>don't miss out</u> on an <u>adventure of a lifetime</u>.
Inform	Camp Townsend is <u>located 45 miles south of Boston</u>. A map <u>will be provided</u> in your <u>camping information packet</u>.
Entertain	Anything that could go wrong did go wrong the summer I attended Camp Townsend. <u>The story goes something like this . . .</u>
Explain	<u>First, put the poles together to make the frame</u> of the tent. Once the frame is together, <u>put the cover on</u> it. The cover should fit snugly. If it doesn't, <u>check the directions again</u> to make sure the frame is properly put together.

Extension Extend the focus on key words that indicate an author's purpose by selecting magazines that are theme based. Have students comb through the articles and other information to find examples of different purposes, including the six purpose words in this activity as well as others that are specifically mentioned in the reading curriculum.

Author's Purpose

Matching Purposes

Procedure   Prepare by writing the statements from the "Topic Descriptions" sheet (provided in Appendix F) on index cards, one statement per card, with a marker. Keep the cards in sets (according to how the statements are designated by group). When finished, you should have made three sets, each set containing five index cards.

Write the following purposes on the board, leaving space underneath each:

Describe   *Persuade*   *Entertain*   *Inform*   *Explain*

Divide the class into three groups. Distribute a set of index cards to each group.

Ask the groups to decide which description of a piece of writing belongs with which purpose for writing.

Assessment   Provide each group with a roll of tape and invite the group members to tape their statements underneath the appropriate purposes for writing listed on the board. Ask groups to "teach" their peers by discussing their reasons for their selections. (See the answer key that follows.)

Ask if there are key words in the topics that provide clues (such as *why* in the persuasive topics and *how to* in the explanatory topics). Have students identify other types of clues that can be observed (such as the persuasive topics are all opinions and the description topics are about how things look).

Tell students that when they encounter questions on reading tests that ask about the author's purpose, they can use these kinds of clues to figure out the correct answers.

Answer Key

Describe: how charming Summit Lake is at sunset; what basset hounds look like; the new design of the voting booths for the school election

Persuade: why Summit Lake is the best vacation spot within a 200-mile radius; why basset hounds are the best medium-size dog to have; why Erma Coffey should win the school election

Entertain: how my father stood up in the fishing boat and dumped us all into the lake; how my dog's tongue drags on the ground after a long walk; how I went blank in the middle of my "Meet the Candidates" speech

Inform: why a dam was constructed at Summit Lake 100 years ago; country of origin and meaning of the words *basset hound*; when and where students can cast their votes in the school election

Explain: how to build a wood canoe for use at Summit Lake; how to groom a basset hound; how to officially get a place on the school election ballot

Author's Purpose/Author's Organization

The Scavenger Hunt

Resources   Literature textbooks; newspapers; magazines

Procedure   Prepare by making copies of the "Scavenger Hunt List" (provided in Appendix F), one for each student.

Announce to students that they will participate in a scavenger hunt. Explain to them that a scavenger hunt involves teams of students on a hunt for specific items on a list; the winning team is the one that collects the most items before the allotted amount of time is reached.

Place students into small groups so that there is an equal number in every group.

Ask all students to have their literature textbooks near them. Also provide access to several newspapers and magazines. Give each group a pad of sticky notes and some pens.

Tell students that you will distribute a scavenger hunt list to each student. Explain that the task is for the group to work together to comb through the text sources to find the items on the list. Each time students find an item, they should use a sticky note to label the text source and attach it to the source. At least one student in each group should record the page number or location of the text source on the scavenger hunt list (so that they will be able to locate the source later).

Distribute a list to each student. Read through each item. Designate the time limit (twenty minutes or so), and tell groups to begin working.

Assessment   When the time is up, ask students to stop working. Ask a group to read off each item found and explain/justify how the text source meets the item description. Have other groups verify if each text source does or does not match the item and keep score on the board. (Contribute to the discussions in order to assess and develop students' understandings of each purpose or organizational pattern on the list.)

Repeat the process until all groups have shared and a winner is determined.

Conclusion

It used to be that campuses felt a slight tremor (usually coming from the administrators' offices) when the testing window in the spring approached. The reality today is that pressure is increasing, and depending on district philosophies, concern about "the test" can be on everyone's lips early in the school year. Consider this: If tests could truly mirror quality instruction and if testing conditions could replicate the collaborative atmosphere that is so important in classrooms, then teachers wouldn't actually need to address "the test" with their students at all; test day could come and go. But that's not what happens with testing. Tests are different from essentially every other activity that takes place in schools. That's why campuses can grow tense.

I think this notion has to be addressed with students explicitly. After all, it must seem odd to them that for many months each school year, they engage with texts and are encouraged to share openly and think broadly about the ideas in those texts, but during test week, they are told not to look around, not to ask around, not to share, and not to think divergently. They must narrow their views. They must limit possible interpretations to a correct one, as deemed by some anonymous test writer.

187

Students need to be privy to honest discussions about tests to minimize their confusion and anxiety about them. They need opportunities to feel prepared and competent not just as learners in classrooms but also as test takers. Confidence comes as a result of a deep awareness of test formats, test language, test tasks, test logic, and other test features that affect students' ability to demonstrate what they know about reading.

Intentions and Reflections

Eliminating students' confusion and anxiety. Helping students feel prepared and competent. Increasing students' confidence. Providing opportunities for students to demonstrate what they know. These are all my main goals for this book.

It is my hope that the various sections and chapters of this book are the beginnings of the ideas, and sometimes the very words, that teachers can share with students. Section 1 seeks to amp up students' ability to work through reading tests both by building the vocabularies they will need and by learning to become savvy in how they navigate tests.

Section 2 aims to help teachers familiarize students with the content of most reading tests; after all, students cannot fully demonstrate what they know when they are confused, anxious, and uncertain about what they will encounter on a test. I tried to fill this section with helpful approaches to taking reading tests, from developing familiarity with item types to having a variety of reading and test-taking strategies that are easy to use.

Section 3 is intended to provide teachers with high-quality content typical of a traditional reading test—materials that might spark rich and lively discussions about test features, tasks, and strategies. The passages and items in this section will, in all hopes, open up opportunities for students to voice their understandings to teachers and for teachers to seize those moments to clarify and develop their students' conceptions.

Section 4 endeavors to supply teachers with engaging activities to strengthen the skills that students will need to demonstrate on most reading tests. As the classroom's decision maker and guide, the teacher can decide how best to present the ideas in the activities—modifying, modeling, and extending the concepts as needed for his or her particular students. The products that students create as a result of completing the activities further provide teachers with access to students' understandings of various reading skills and strategies.

The content of this book grew and grew as I kept returning to the title: *What Every Middle School Teacher Needs to Know About Reading Tests*. The pages represent what I believe is the most important and most useable knowledge for teachers.

Moving Forward and Staying Informed

There are many opportunities that exist beyond this book for teachers to complement and increase their knowledge of tests and testing. One source is e-mail lists that are tailored to providing specific information that is important to you. Your state education department's curriculum and assessment divisions, for example, might have e-mail lists that will deliver valuable information to your inbox. Staying connected to the curriculum and assessment divisions means being reassured that you are being provided with the latest information regarding your state's testing program.

Another source is professional reading organizations that allow members to join e-mail lists that relate specifically to their teaching positions and areas of interest.

Perhaps the best way to stay informed is to visit your state education department Web site. These sites are usually well maintained. Released tests, sample item booklets, and various testing information bulletins can be downloaded from the sites. Because information is made available at various points throughout the school year, it is important to visit regularly.

Letting Your Voice Be Heard

Teachers can and should have their voices heard, within the walls of their school as well as across the state.

On the local level, share. If you've had years of experience with testing and have learned a few things the hard way, share with anyone who will listen eagerly. If you feel in the dark about matters related to testing, listen to anyone who is eager to share. Form a discussion group and work chapter by chapter through this book and others that address topics that are important to you. Agree, disagree, and exemplify your opinions with your classroom experiences.

On the state level, volunteer. State assessments cannot be developed without teacher input. State departments of education seek teachers to volunteer to serve on various committees—from deciding which standards should be assessed in a new testing program to determining which items are appropriate for inclusion on a field test or live administration. In addition to contributing what you know, you will have the opportunity to learn from fellow educators and to receive information directly from the state department staff who are present in these meetings (rather than having to depend on other, sometimes less reliable, channels).

✓ ✓ ✓

Finally, I suppose I should address the elephant in the room. While it is my experience as a test developer that qualified me most for writing this book, it has not been lost on me that readers may think that my experience in the industry inevitably makes me a proponent of testing. The simple truth is that I do think that assessments of various types can provide useful data, but I also know that test scores are being valued presently on local, state, and national levels in ways that fall outside the purposes and legitimacy of those tests.

I want teachers to have the information in this book so that tests are less powerful, not more powerful. I want this book to be a resource for teachers to draw on during their delivery of high-quality instruction, not a prescriptive plan that reduces classrooms to dens of test practice. I want teachers to decide what they think their students should know about reading tests and to decide how students should receive that information so that they feel informed, prepared, competent, and capable.

Knowledge about reading tests wipes out the mystery of them. Knowledge about reading tests lessens fear and concern. Knowledge about reading tests prevents the further confiscating of valuable instructional time with students.

Neither teacher nor student should feel defenseless as the test day arrives.

Appendix A:
Vocabulary Development

Context Clues Search Results

Title of Text: **Sentence containing unfamiliar word:** **Context clues:** **Guessed meaning:** **Dictionary meaning:**	**Title of Text:** **Sentence containing unfamiliar word:** **Context clues:** **Guessed meaning:** **Dictionary meaning:**
Title of Text: **Sentence containing unfamiliar word:** **Context clues:** **Guessed meaning:** **Dictionary meaning:**	**Title of Text:** **Sentence containing unfamiliar word:** **Context clues:** **Guessed meaning:** **Dictionary meaning:**

Breakup Cards

Attentive	Showing attention
Clarify	To make clear(er)
Contradict	To say something against or opposite of
Decoration	The results of being decorated
Disharmonious	Not having harmony
Disorder	Not orderly
Dreadful	Full of dread
Evaluation	The results of measuring the value of something
Extract	Pull/drag from
Gloomy	Having gloom
Gradually	In a gradual manner
Harmless	Without harm
Hypersensitive	Having an extra capacity to feel
Imperfection	The results of not being perfect
Impossible	Not possible
Inscription	The results of writing in or on something

Breakup Cards *(continued)*

Invalid	Not strong
Irresistible	Not able to be resisted
Knowledgeable	Having knowledge
Manuscript	Writing done by hand
Meaningless	Having no meaning
Memorial	Something made or done to remember a person or event
Nonsense	Without sense
Peacefully	In the manner of having peace
Portable	Able to be carried
Preview	To view before
Revive	To bring back to living
Simplify	To make simple(r)
Spectacle	Relating to looking or seeing
Telegram	A written message sent from a distance
Unapproachable	Not able to approach
Unashamed	Not ashamed

Connotation Squares

Group 1

Classic	Ancient	Timeless	Old
Antiquated	Mature	Experienced	Veteran
Seasoned	Aged	Has-been	Old-fashioned

Group 2

Frugal	Stingy	Selfish	Cheap
Tightwad	Cautious	Tightfisted	Miserly
Thrifty	Prudent	Economical	Sensible
Practical	Wise	Conservative	Reasonable

Group 3

Spirited	Bratty	Lively	Misbehaved
Energetic	Active	Spoiled	Naughty

Appendix B:
Important Ideas

Story Windows

Appendix C:
Literary Elements

Character Traits

active	creative	hardworking	practical
adventurous	critical	hateful	protective
afraid	curious	honorable	proud
alone	daring	hopeful/-less	pushy
amazed	dedicated	humorous	puzzled
ambitious	delighted	imaginative	quiet
amused	demanding	(im)mature	regretful
angry	dependent	(im)patient	relaxed
annoyed/-ing	desperate	independent	reluctant
anxious	determined	innocent	respected
appreciative	disappointed	inspired	responsible
apprehensive	(dis)honest	intelligent	satisfied
ashamed	disorganized	interested	scared
astonished	doubtful	irritated	secretive
attentive	eager	joyful	selfish/selfless
awed	embarrassed	kind/unkind	sensible
bashful	encouraged	lazy	serious
bewildered	energetic	lonely	shocked
bold	envious	lucky	sincere
bored	excited	mad	skilled
bossy	fair/unfair	mean	startled
bothered	fearful/-less	melancholy	stubborn
bothersome	forceful	motivated	stunned
brave	fortunate	mysterious	sure/unsure
bright	frantic	negative	surprised
calm	frightened	nervous	suspicious
careful/-less	frustrated	noble	sympathetic
caring	funny	offended	talented
certain	furious	optimistic	thoughtful/-less
cheerful	generous	overwhelmed	thrilled
childish	giving	particular	timid
clever	glad	passionate	troubled
concerned	gloomy	perplexed	trustworthy
confident	gracious	picky	truthful
confused	grateful	plain	understanding
content	greedy	playful	upset
courageous	guilty	pleased	weak
cowardly	happy/unhappy	polite	worried

What Every Middle School Teacher Needs to Know About Reading Tests (From Someone Who Has Written Them) by Charles Fuhrken. Copyright © 2012. Stenhouse Publishers.

Character-logue Sample

Speaker 1: What happened earlier today?

Speaker 2: A boy slipped off the edge of the bank. The river was rushing wildly. People were screaming, "The boy fell in! The boy fell in!"

Speaker 1: So then what happened?

Speaker 2: Without a second thought, I jumped in after him. I'm not the best swimmer, but I knew a kid that young wouldn't have the strength to fight the current.

Speaker 1: Were you able to save him?

Speaker 2: Yes. When I reached him, I told him to hold on to my T-shirt, and I swam to a rock and lifted him on top of it. We stayed there until rescue workers could help us.

Speaker 1: So that's why people are calling you _____.

Trait Description Outline

My name is _____ (character trait).

Today was a _____ day.

Getting ready for school today, _____.

During _____ class, _____.

At lunch, _____.

In the hallway, _____.

After school, _____.

That is what life is like when you're _____
(character trait).

What Every Middle School Teacher Needs to Know About Reading Tests (From Someone Who Has Written Them) by Charles Fuhrken. Copyright © 2012. Stenhouse Publishers.

Trait Description for *Distant*

My name is *Distant*.

Today was a rather lonely day, but I made it that way.

Getting ready for school today, I stayed in my room until it was time to leave so that I wouldn't have to talk to my sister at the breakfast table.

During math class, I chose to do my work alone even though the teacher said we could work in groups.

At lunch, my friend Cynthia waved me over to sit with her at the picnic table, but I wanted to sit under a shade tree by myself.

In the hallway, I kept my head down and went directly to my classes instead of hanging out until the tardy bell rang.

After school, I went to my room and put on my headphones so I could listen to music until the day was done.

That is what life is like when you're *distant*.

What Every Middle School Teacher Needs to Know About Reading Tests (From Someone Who Has Written Them) by Charles Fuhrken. Copyright © 2012. Stenhouse Publishers.

Graphic Organizer About Lance Armstrong

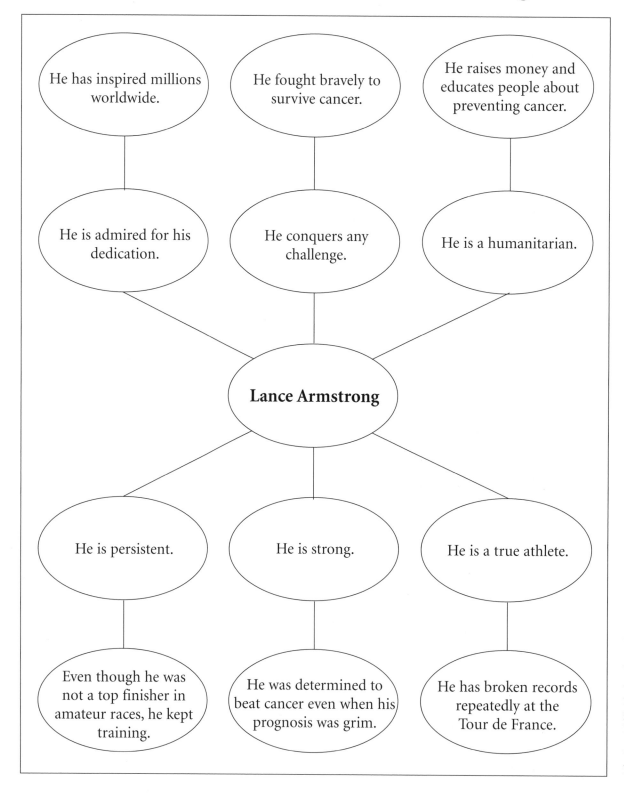

Found Poem

The Indian Dog

I bought a dog, a bargain at five dollars.
It belonged to a Navajo man.

It was an unremarkable creature, but full of
resistance with a deep, abiding
love for its previous owner.

I secured my dog the first
night but his will helped him
escape, helped him
return to his previous life, teaching me
a lesson about where its heart
longed
to be.

Appendix D:
Literary Techniques

Anchor Examples for Literary Techniques

Idiomatic/Figurative Language Definition: Examples:	**Simile** Definition: Examples:
Metaphor Definition: Examples:	**Personification** Definition: Examples:
Hyperbole Definition: Examples:	**Analogy** Definition: Examples:
Mood Definition: Examples:	**Tone** Definition: Examples:

What Every Middle School Teacher Needs to Know About Reading Tests (From Someone Who Has Written Them) by Charles Fuhrken. Copyright © 2012. Stenhouse Publishers.

Nonhuman Subjects and Human Verbs

Nonhuman Subjects	Human Verbs
thoughts	danced
ideas	whispered
truth	spoke
doubt	moaned
memories	cried
rain	called out
breeze	ate
wind	awoke
clouds	slept
lightning	raced
thunder	skipped
tree	ran
hurricane	walked
tornado	hurried
fire	huddled
flames	shook
dessert	cradled
dirty dishes	wrapped
sun	agreed
moon	refused
stars	angered
sky	applauded
mountains	remembered

Excerpt from Carl Sandburg's Poem "Yarns"

They have yarns . . .

Of pancakes so thin they had only one side, . . .

Of the old man's whiskers: "When the wind was with him his whiskers arrived a day before he did," . . .

Of railroad trains whizzing along so fast they reached the station before the whistle.

What Every Middle School Teacher Needs to Know About Reading Tests (From Someone Who Has Written Them) by Charles Fuhrken. Copyright © 2012. Stenhouse Publishers.

Hyperbole Starters

Example: Marissa really loved the movie.	Example: She talked about it nonstop for two days.
That cookie recipe was too complicated.	
It was so cold yesterday.	
The hurricane was brutal.	
I miss my friend who moved away.	
The librarian demands absolute silence in the library—or else!	
My backpack has so much stuff in it.	
The play by Shakespeare was so boring.	
The ant colony in my backyard is huge.	
The popcorn had too much butter on it.	

Teacher's Guide for Hyperbole Starters

That cookie recipe was too complicated.	It required about a hundred ingredients.
It was so cold yesterday.	Even the burning wood in the fireplace had icicles hanging from it.
The hurricane was brutal.	It blew our little Texas town into the state of Oregon.
I miss my friend who moved away.	I think of her two million times a day.
The librarian demands absolute silence in the library—or else!	Even a mouse is scared to go there.
My backpack has so much stuff in it.	I had to hire a professional weightlifter to carry it for me.
The play by Shakespeare was so boring.	The audience's snores were so loud that we couldn't hear the actors.
The ant colony in my backyard is huge.	The city has decided to give it a zip code.
The popcorn had too much butter on it.	I didn't get to eat a single bite because the popcorn kept slipping through my fingers.

What Every Middle School Teacher Needs to Know About Reading Tests (From Someone Who Has Written Them) by Charles Fuhrken. Copyright © 2012. Stenhouse Publishers.

Really Bad Analogies

She had a deep, throaty, genuine laugh, like that sound a dog makes just before it throws up.

Her hair glistened in the rain like a nose hair after a sneeze.

The young fighter had a hungry look, the kind you get from not eating for a while.

It was an American tradition, like fathers chasing kids around with power tools.

He was deeply in love. When she spoke, he thought he heard bells, as if she were a garbage truck backing up.

Source: *Washington Post Style Invitational* (1999)

Moods and Tones

Moods	Tones
Playful	Formal
Mysterious	Objective/Unbiased/Neutral
Suspenseful	Informal/Friendly
Tense	Critical
Triumphant	Persuasive
Anxious	Candid/Matter-of-Fact
Uncertain	Apologetic
Disappointed	Sympathetic
Anticipatory	Sentimental
Urgent	Humorous/Joking/Lighthearted
Sad/Regretful	Detached/Indifferent
Pessimistic	Dramatic
Melancholic	Angry/Bitter
Mournful/Sorrowful	Curious
Optimistic	Regretful
Foreboding/Apprehensive	Urgent
Joyful/Celebratory	Serious

Style Excerpts

The man lowered the bullhorn and glared. There were giggles and flinches, but no one broke.
    "Get . . . *set*!"
    Glare. Silence. Eyes. Bullhorn. Wait. Wait. You could almost hear the eggs.
	Eggs everywhere! Sky blue. Pink. Yellow. Lilac. Pastel treasures in a shaggy grass pie.
	    There were too many. He wanted them all. He wanted piles. He wanted armloads. He could not aim his attention at only one. He could not pick out the first.

He kept hearing his mother's voice, calling him from the top of a sunlit hill. . . . He saw leaves, a figure darkly rising, shedding dry leaves, rising silently as moss in wooden silence, and he tried and tried but he could not see her face.	David took it and walked away. And now he wondered: Why? Why had he asked for it? What was he going to do with it? He didn't know. He stared at the picture. Could he be wrong?
Weeks went by. A month. Two. School was out. David had stopped searching the newspaper.	He put on his yo-yo belt and holster, posed himself like a gunfighter, told her to count to three, and showed her how fast he could whip out his many-colored Spitfire and skin the cat.
They talked because it was night, and because weird people walk the tracks at night, and because there was nothing else to do, and because they could barely see each other, and because maybe the bushes were not enough.	"Don't wait up," Primrose sang. "I'm not kidding, missy." "I *heard* you."
They lived in the same town, but only the sky was vast enough to measure the distance between them.	"I'm not," said the lady. Her tongue, like a nightcrawler, slid out, poked around her upper lip till the yellow spot was gone—*htthhhp*—back into its hole.

And for the rest of her life she would smugly believe she had successfully punished then pardoned him. He could not allow it.
    Think. Think.
    He went into the kitchen and got a Mango Madness from the refrigerator.
	"Heck no. You want to hunt for deer, there's a special season. Bears? Special season. Pheasants? Special season. Worms?" she shone the red light in his face.
	    "Special season?"

Source: *Eggs* by Jerry Spinelli (2007)

Style Descriptions

Using sound imagery	Presenting a long, fluid, one-sentence paragraph that allows the reader to picture the scene
Using descriptive language to set a scene	Using short, rhythmic, patterned sentences
Using figurative language/personification to emphasize an important idea	Using a series of short sentences to emphasize the passing of time
Establishing a pattern and then breaking it	Stopping the action with a one-word sentence that is repeated; using italics to show someone's thinking
Using one-word sentences to slow down a scene	Using questions that show a character's uncertain thoughts
Stringing related ideas together with particular words	Using italics for emphasis

Teacher's Guide for "You've Got Style"

What Every Middle School Teacher Needs to Know About Reading Tests (From Someone Who Has Written Them) by Charles Fuhrken. Copyright © 2012. Stenhouse Publishers.

The man lowered the bullhorn and glared. There were giggles and flinches, but no one broke.
    "Get . . . *set!*"
    Glare. Silence. Eyes. Bullhorn. Wait. Wait. You could almost hear the eggs.
 	
(Using one-word sentences to slow down a scene)
	Eggs everywhere! Sky blue. Pink. Yellow. Lilac. Pastel treasures in a shaggy grass pie.
	    There were too many. He wanted them all. He wanted piles. He wanted armloads. He could not aim his attention at only one. He could not pick out the first.
	(Using short, rhythmic, patterned sentences)

He kept hearing his mother's voice, calling him from the top of a sunlit hill. . . . He saw leaves, a figure darkly rising, shedding dry leaves, rising silently as moss in wooden silence, and he tried and tried but he could not see her face. *(Using descriptive language to set a scene)*	David took it and walked away. And now he wondered: Why? Why had he asked for it? What was he going to do with it? He didn't know. He stared at the picture. Could he be wrong? *(Using questions that show a character's uncertain thoughts)*
Weeks went by. A month. Two. School was out. David had stopped searching the newspaper. *(Using a series of short sentences to emphasize the passing of time)*	He put on his yo-yo belt and holster, posed himself like a gunfighter, told her to count to three, and showed her how fast he could whip out his many-colored Spitfire and skin the cat. *(Presenting a long, fluid, one-sentence paragraph that allows the reader to picture the scene)*

They talked because it was night, and because weird people walk the tracks at night, and because there was nothing else to do, and because they could barely see each other, and because maybe the bushes were not enough.
 	
(Stringing related ideas together with particular words)
	"Don't wait up," Primrose sang.
	    "I'm not kidding, missy."
	    "I *heard* you."
	
	(Using italics for emphasis)

They lived in the same town, but only the sky was vast enough to measure the distance between them. *(Using figurative language/personification to emphasize an important idea)*	"I'm not," said the lady. Her tongue, like a nightcrawler, slid out, poked around her upper lip till the yellow spot was gone—*htthhhp*—back into its hole. *(Using sound imagery)*

And for the rest of her life she would smugly believe she had successfully punished then pardoned him. He could not allow it.
    Think. Think.
    He went into the kitchen and got a Mango Madness from the refrigerator.
(Stopping the action with a one-word sentence that is repeated; using italics to show someone's thinking)
	"Heck no. You want to hunt for deer, there's a special season. Bears? Special season. Pheasants? Special season. Worms?" she shone the red light in his face.
	    "Special season?"
	
	(Establishing a pattern and then breaking it)

Source: *Eggs* by Jerry Spinelli (2007)

Appendix E:
Interpretations

Jumbled Fiction Sentences

But when his family moved to a new town, Joseph was in for a surprise.

So when Steve "Big Bones" Bradford made Joseph the water boy during his first attempt to join the boys for football, Joseph complied eagerly.

Joseph wasn't usually the kind of guy who took orders from other neighborhood kids.

Of those who congregated on his block to play ball, he was the tallest by at least a foot and outweighed most by more than 50 pounds.

He hoped that eventually, with more time hanging out with these guys, he'd earn a more important position.

Usually he was the kind who gave them.

He was now the youngest of the neighborhood boys, and he looked rail-thin up against those older boys.

Jumbled Nonfiction Sentences

The earliest known reference to the idea is in a letter written in 1754 by Englishman William Stukeley; he refers to the Great Wall of China as a "considerable figure" and one that "may be discerned at the moon."
But is the wall so imposing in stature that it can be seen from the moon?
Being able to see the width of the wall from the moon would be about the same as being able to see a human hair from two miles away!
No.
There is no question that the Great Wall of China is an impressive structure.
It turns out, then, that the belief has achieved urban legend status even today as a way of memorializing this most impressive structure built by hand so many centuries ago.
Renewed interest in the possibility occurred when a 1932 cartoon theorized that the Great Wall was ". . . the mightiest work of man, the only one that would be visible to the human eye from the moon."
Obviously, the best way to know for certain whether the wall is visible from the moon would be to travel to the moon and look!
That notion was debated for years.
Just a few years later, in 1938, the claim appeared to have more scientific support when Richard Halliburton included the thought in his book *Second Book of Marvels*.
So, has any astronaut ever claimed to have seen the Great Wall of China while on the moon?

Answer Key for "Jumbled Fiction Sentences" and "Jumbled Nonfiction Sentences"

Jumbled Fiction Sentences, in Their Proper Sequence

(1) Joseph wasn't usually the kind of guy who took orders from other neighborhood kids.

(2) Usually he was the kind who gave them.

(3) Of those who congregated on his block to play ball, he was the tallest by at least a foot and outweighed most by more than 50 pounds.

(4) But when his family moved to a new town, Joseph was in for a surprise.

(5) He was now the youngest of the neighborhood boys, and he looked rail-thin up against those older boys.

(6) So when Steve "Big Bones" Bradford made Joseph the water boy during his first attempt to join the boys for football, Joseph complied eagerly.

(7) He hoped that eventually, with more time hanging out with these guys, he'd earn a more important position.

Jumbled Nonfiction Sentences, in Their Proper Sequence

(1) There is no question that the Great Wall of China is an impressive structure.

(2) But is the wall so imposing in stature that it can be seen from the moon?

(3) That notion was debated for years.

(4) The earliest known reference to the idea is in a letter written in 1754 by Englishman William Stukeley; he refers to the Great Wall of China as a "considerable figure" and one that "may be discerned at the moon."

(5) Renewed interest in the possibility occurred when a 1932 cartoon theorized that the Great Wall was ". . . the mightiest work of man, the only one that would be visible to the human eye from the moon."

(6) Just a few years later, in 1938, the claim appeared to have more scientific support when Richard Halliburton included the thought in his book *Second Book of Marvels*.

(7) Obviously, the best way to know for certain whether the wall is visible from the moon would be to travel to the moon and look!

(8) So, has any astronaut ever claimed to have seen the Great Wall of China while on the moon?

(9) No.

(10) Being able to see the width of the wall from the moon would be about the same as being able to see a human hair from two miles away!

(11) It turns out, then, that the belief has achieved urban legend status even today as a way of memorializing this most impressive structure built by hand so many centuries ago.

What Every Middle School Teacher Needs to Know About Reading Tests (From Someone Who Has Written Them) by Charles Fuhrken. Copyright © 2012. Stenhouse Publishers.

Things to Compare in Fiction Passages

Setting	• How are the settings alike or different? • What effect does the setting have on each passage?
Plot	• What are the significant events in each passage? • How are the most significant events in each passage alike or different?
Characters	• In what ways are the characters alike or different? • How do the characters behave? What do they say and do? How do they feel? Do the characters change?
Problem	• What problems are the characters facing? • How are the problems alike or different? • How does the reader learn about the problems?
Solution	• How does a character try to solve his or her problem? • What solution satisfies the character?
Theme	• What big idea(s) does the reader walk away with? • What can the reader learn as a result of having read about the characters?
Point of View	• From what point of view is each passage told? • What effect does the point of view have on the passage?
Organization and Type	• How are the events told? • What type of text is each passage?
Technique	• What is special about how the author presents each passage?

Things to Compare in Nonfiction Passages

Topic/ Information	• What information is the same and different in the passages? • Is any information emphasized differently in the passages?
Facts/Opinions	• Is the information presented mostly facts, opinions, or a combination? • What effect does the type of information presented have on the passage?
Organization	• How is the information presented in the passages? (cause-effect, problem-solution, main ideas–supporting examples, etc.) • Does the author use any special features (such as subheadings or photographs)?
Tone	• Is the author's attitude about the topic of the passages evident?
Purpose	• What is the author's purpose in writing about the topic?
Style	• Does the author present the information in the passages in special ways (such as using questions, talking directly to the reader, or using descriptive language)?

What Every Middle School Teacher Needs to Know About Reading Tests (From Someone Who Has Written Them) by Charles Fuhrken. Copyright © 2012. Stenhouse Publishers.

Says and Feels

"I won't be as pleasant the next time you show up late, young man."	Annoyed
"I had no idea that you were planning a party for me."	Surprised
"Can we mow the grass later, Dad? I don't feel like it right now."	Tired
"I'm doing the jump because it hasn't been done before. If it had, it wouldn't be as fun!"	Daring
"How nice of you to help me with my homework this afternoon."	Appreciative
"We need a fund-raising plan that will make the most amount of money with the least amount of effort."	Sensible
"I just couldn't get out of bed all weekend. I can't imagine that my friendship with Katie is over."	Gloomy
"I know that it means not having a free Saturday for the next three months, but I'm willing to make that commitment to help the people of my community."	Hardworking
"I had no intention of sharing the reward money. It's mine."	Selfish

Says and Feels *(continued)*

"I don't even know why other people enter this contest. I'm much more experienced and talented than they."	Arrogant
"I cannot believe the package hasn't arrived. I could spit nails."	Furious
"Don't put the books back on the shelf. I want them placed there in a certain way."	Particular
"I just wanted the earth to swallow me up."	Embarrassed
"Justin had no business being in the building that early. I'm thinking he was up to something."	Suspicious
"You'll have to drive faster. I simply must get to the auditorium within the next ten minutes!"	Frantic
"I couldn't imagine being on stage by myself, so I grabbed Eric's arm and pulled him up there with me!"	Bashful
"Since we ran out of time today in the seminar, do you think I could e-mail you a few more of my questions, Mr. Ree?"	Interested
"When I didn't see my name on the award list, I just stood there, unable to move."	Shocked

Appendix F:
Text Matters

Purposes and Examples

Describe	Camp Townsend is located on the banks of a sparkling blue river and nestled between two beautifully wooded mountains.
List	Each camper is responsible for the following: snacks and water, hiking boots, a fishing pole, a backpack, and a sleeping bag.
Persuade/Convince	You must join us this weekend; don't miss out on an adventure of a lifetime.
Inform	Camp Townsend is located 45 miles south of Boston. A map will be provided in your camping information packet.
Entertain	Anything that could go wrong did go wrong the summer I attended Camp Townsend. The story goes something like this . . .
Explain	First, put the poles together to make the frame of the tent. After the frame is together, put the cover on it. The cover should fit snugly. If it doesn't, check the directions again to make sure the frame is properly put together.

Topic Descriptions

Group 1

how charming Summit Lake is at sunset

how to build a wood canoe for use at Summit Lake

why Summit Lake is the best vacation spot within a 200-mile radius

why a dam was constructed at Summit Lake 100 years ago

how my father stood up in the fishing boat and dumped us all into
the lake

Group 2

what basset hounds look like

how to groom a basset hound

why basset hounds are the best medium-size dog to have

country of origin and meaning of the words *basset hound*

how my dog's tongue drags on the ground after a long walk

Group 3

the new design of the voting booths for the school election

how to officially get a place on the school election ballot

why Erma Coffey should win the school election

when and where students can cast their votes in the school election

how I went blank in the middle of my "Meet the Candidates" speech

What Every Middle School Teacher Needs to Know About Reading Tests (From Someone Who Has Written Them) by Charles Fuhrken. Copyright © 2012. Stenhouse Publishers.

Scavenger Hunt List

1. An advertisement that uses persuasive language

2. An article, essay, or editorial in which the main purpose is to express an opinion

3. A piece of writing with a focus on conveying information without bias

4. A poem meant to express emotions

5. A story told in chronological order

6. A myth, legend, or tale that is intended to teach a lesson

7. A piece of writing that explains something with a list or steps

8. Nonfiction writing with a cause-effect structure

9. Nonfiction writing that uses subheadings as an organizational structure

10. Nonfiction writing that begins with a series of questions, an interesting comparison, or a startling fact

Calkins, Lucy, Kate Montgomery, and Donna Santman. 1998. *A Teacher's Guide to Standardized Reading Tests: Knowledge Is Power.* Portsmouth, NH: Heinemann.

Conrad, Lori L., Missy Matthews, Cheryl Zimmerman, and Patrick A. Allen. 2008. *Put Thinking to the Test.* Portland, ME: Stenhouse.

Downing, Steven M., and Thomas M. Haladyna. 2006. *Handbook of Test Development.* Mahwah, NJ: Lawrence Erlbaum.

Firestone, William A., Roberta Y. Schorr, and Lora F. Monfils. 2004. *The Ambiguity of Teaching to the Test: Standards, Assessment, and Educational Reform.* Mahwah, NJ: Lawrence Erlbaum.

Fuhrken, Charles, and Nancy Roser. 2010. "Exploring High-Stakes Tests as a Genre." In *Teaching New Literacies in Grades 4–6.* Ed. Barbara Moss and Diane Lapp. New York: Guilford.

Gallagher, Kelly. 2009. *Readicide: How Schools Are Killing Reading and What You Can Do About It.* Portland, ME: Stenhouse.

Greene, Amy H., and Glennon D. Melton. 2007. *Test Talk: Integrating Test Preparation into Reading Workshop.* Portland, ME: Stenhouse.

Johnson, Genevieve. 1998. "Principles of Instruction for At-Risk Learners." *Preventing School Failure* 4: 167–174.

Kohn, Alfie. 2000. *The Case Against Standardized Testing: Raising the Scores, Ruining the Schools.* Portsmouth, NH: Heinemann.

Pearson, P. David, and Margaret C. Gallagher. 1983. "The Instruction of Reading Comprehension." *Contemporary Educational Psychology* 8: 317–344.

Santman, Donna. 2002. "Teaching to the Test?: Test Preparation in the Reading Workshop." *Language Arts* 79: 203–211.

Serafini, Frank. 2004. *Lessons in Comprehension: Explicit Instruction in the Reading Workshop.* Portsmouth, NH: Heinemann.

Smith, Michael W., and Jeffrey D. Wilhelm. 2002. *"Reading Don't Fix No Chevys": Literacy in the Lives of Young Men.* Portsmouth, NH: Heinemann.

Valencia, Richard R., and Bruno J. Villarreal. 2003. "Improving Students' Reading Performance via Standards-based School Reform: A Critique." *The Reading Teacher* 56: 612–621.

Vygotsky, Lev S. 1978. *Mind in Society: Development of Higher Psychological Processes.* Cambridge, MA: Harvard University Press.

Washington Post Style Invitational. 1999. Reprinted with commentary in "Writing English: The International Language of Business." http://www.writingenglish.wordpress.com/2006/09/12.

Literature

Ahlberg, Allan. 2007. *Previously.* Cambridge, MA: Candlewick.

Bauer, Joan. 1998. *Rules of the Road.* New York: Penguin.

Cofer, Judith Ortiz. 1995. "An Hour with Abuelo." In *An Island Like You.* New York: Orchard Books.

Gaskill, Melissa. 2005. "Bad Sports." *Texas Co-op Power: A Magazine About Texas Living* 62 (2): 20–21.

McDonald, Walt. 2005. "No Matter Where You've Been." *Texas Co-op Power: A Magazine About Texas Living* 61 (8): 38.

Momaday, N. Scott. 1998. "The Indian Dog." In *The Man Made of Words: Essays, Stories, Passages.* New York: St. Martin's.

Nye, Naomi S. 2000. *Come With Me: Poems for a Journey.* New York: HarperCollins.

Prelutsky, Jack. 1990. *Something Big Has Been Here.* New York: Greenwillow Books.

Sandburg, Carl. 1964. *The People, Yes.* New York: Harcourt.

Spinelli, Jerry. 2007. *Eggs.* New York: Little, Brown.